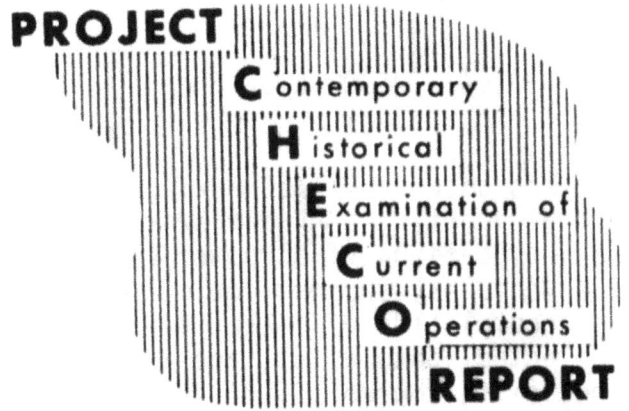

PROJECT CHECO REPORT
Contemporary Historical Examination of Current Operations

VNAF IMPROVEMENT AND MODERNIZATION PROGRAM (U)

5 FEBRUARY 1970

HQ PACAF

Directorate, Tactical Evaluation
CHECO Division

Prepared by:

MR JAMES T. BEAR

Project CHECO 7th AF, DOAC

PROJECT CHECO REPORTS

The counterinsurgency and unconventional warfare environment of Southeast Asia has resulted in the employment of USAF airpower to meet a multitude of requirements. The varied applications of airpower have involved the full spectrum of USAF aerospace vehicles, support equipment, and manpower. As a result, there has been an accumulation of operational data and experiences that, as a priority, must be collected, documented, and analyzed as to current and future impact upon USAF policies, concepts, and doctrine.

Fortunately, the value of collecting and documenting our SEA experiences was recognized at an early date. In 1962, Hq USAF directed CINCPACAF to establish an activity that would be primarily responsive to Air Staff requirements and direction, and would provide timely and analytical studies of USAF combat operations in SEA.

Project CHECO, an acronym for Contemporary Historical Examination of Current Operations, was established to meet this Air Staff requirement. Managed by Hq PACAF, with elements at Hq 7AF and 7AF/13AF, Project CHECO provides a scholarly, "on-going" historical examination, documentation, and reporting on USAF policies, concepts, and doctrine in PACOM. This CHECO report is part of the overall documentation and examination which is being accomplished. Along with the other CHECO publications, this is an authentic source for an assessment of the effectiveness of USAF airpower in PACOM.

MILTON B. ADAMS, Major General, USAF
Chief of Staff

REPLY TO
ATTN OF: DOVD

5 February 1970

SUBJECT: Project CHECO Report, "VNAF Improvement and Modernization Program" (U)

TO: SEE DISTRIBUTION PAGE

1. Attached is a SECRET NOFORN document. It shall be transported, stored, safeguarded, and accounted for in accordance with applicable security directives. SPECIAL HANDLING REQUIRED, NOT RELEASABLE TO FOREIGN NATIONALS. The information contained in this document will not be disclosed to foreign nationals or their representatives. Retain or destroy in accordance with AFR 205-1. Do not return.

2. This letter does not contain classified information and may be declassified if attachment is removed from it.

FOR THE COMMANDER IN CHIEF

MAURICE L. GRIFFITH, Colonel, USAF
Chief, CHECO Division
Directorate, Tactical Evaluation
DCS/Operations

1 Atch
Proj CHECO Rprt (S/NF),
5 Feb 70

DISTRIBUTION LIST

1. SECRETARY OF THE AIR FORCE

    a. SAFAA 1
    b. SAFLL 1
    c. SAFOI 2

2. HEADQUARTERS USAF

    a. AFBSA 1

    b. AFCCS
        (1) AFCCSSA 1
        (2) AFCVC 1
        (3) AFCAV 1
        (4) AFCHO 2

    c. AFCSA
        (1) AFCSAG 1
        (2) AFCSAMI 1

    d. AFGOA 2

    e. AFIGO
        (1) AFISI 3
        (2) AFISP 1

    f. AFMSG 1

    g. AFNIATC 5

    h. AFAAC 1
        (1) AFAMAI 1

    i. AFODC
        (1) AFOAP 1
        (2) AFOCC 1
        (3) AFOCE 1
        (5) AFOMO 1

    j. AFPDC
        (1) AFPDPSS 1
        (2) AFPMDG 1
        (3) AFPDW 1

    k. AFRDC 1
        (1) AFRDD 1
        (2) AFRDQ 1
        (3) AFRDQRC 1
        (4) AFRDR 1

    l. AFSDC
        (1) AFSLP 1
        (2) AFSME 1
        (3) AFSMS 1
        (4) AFSPD 1
        (5) AFSSS 1
        (6) AFSTP 1

    m. AFTAC 1

    n. AFXDC 1
        (1) AFXDO 1
        (2) AFXDOC 1
        (3) AFXDOD 1
        (4) AFXDOL 1
        (5) AFXOP 1
        (6) AFXOSL 1
        (7) AFXOSN 1
        (8) AFXOSO 1
        (9) AFXOSS 1
        (10) AFXOSV 1
        (11) AFXOTR 1
        (12) AFXOTW 1
        (13) AFXOTZ 1
        (14) AFXOXY 1
        (15) AFXPD 6
            (a) AFXPPGS 3

3. MAJOR COMMANDS

   a. TAC

      (1) HEADQUARTERS
          (a) DO. 1
          (b) DPL 2
          (c) DOCC. 1
          (d) DOREA 1
          (e) DIO 1

      (2) AIR FORCES
          (a) 12AF
              1. DORF 1
              2. DI 1
          (b) 19AF(DI). 1
          (c) USAFSOF(DO) 1

      (3) WINGS
          (a) 1SOW(DOI) 1
          (b) 4TFW(DO). 1
          (c) 23TFW(DOI). 1
          (d) 27TFW(DOI). 1
          (e) 33TFW(DOI). 1
          (f) 64TAW(DOI). 1
          (g) 67TRW(C). 1
          (h) 75TRW(DOI). 1
          (i) 316TAW(DOP) 1
          (j) 317TAW(EX). 1
          (k) 363TRW(DOI) 1
          (l) 464TAW(DOIN). 1
          (m) 474TFW(TFOX). 1
          (n) 479TFW(DOF) 1
          (o) 516TAW(DOPL). 1
          (p) 4410CCTW(DOTR). . . . 1
          (q) 58TFTW(I) 1
          (r) 4554CCTW(DOI) 1

      (4) TAC CENTERS, SCHOOLS
          (a) USAFTAWC(DA) 2
          (b) USAFTARC(DID) . . . 2
          (c) USAFTALC(DCRL). . . 1
          (d) USAFTFWC(CRCD). . . 1

          (e) USAFAGOS(DAB-C) . . . 1

   b. SAC

      (1) HEADQUARTERS
          (a) DOPL. 1
          (b) DPLF. 1
          (c) DM. 1
          (d) DI. 1
          (e) OA. 1
          (f) HI. 1

      (2) AIR FORCES
          (a) 2AF(DICS) 1
          (b) 8AF(DO) 3
          (c) 15AF(DI). 1

   c. MAC

      (1) HEADQUARTERS
          (a) MAOID 1
          (b) MAOCO 1
          (c) MACHO 1
          (d) MACOA 1

      (2) AIR FORCES
          (a) 22AF(OCXI). 1

      (3) WINGS
          (a) 61MAWg(OIN) 1
          (b) 62MAWg(OXCP). 1
          (c) 436MAWg(OXCX) 1
          (d) 437MAWg(OCXI) 1
          (e) 438MAWg(OCXC) 1

      (4) MAC SERVICES
          (a) AWS(AWCHO). 1
          (b) ARRS(ARXLR) 1
          (c) ACGS(AGOV). 1

d. ADC

    (1) HEADQUARTERS
        (a) ADODC 1
        (b) ADOOP 1
        (c) ADLCC 1

    (2) AIR DIVISIONS
        (a) 25AD(OIN) 1
        (b) 29AD(ODC) 1
        (c) 20AD(OIN) 1

e. ATC

    (1) HEADQUARTERS
        (a) ATXPP-X 1

f. AFLC

    (1) HEADQUARTERS
        (a) MCVSS 1

g. AFSC

    (1) HEADQUARTERS
        (a) SCLAP 3
        (b) SCS-6 1
        (c) SCGCH 2
        (d) SCTPL 1
        (e) ASD(ASJT) 1
        (f) ESD(ESO) 1
        (g) RADC(EMOEL) 2
        (h) ADTC(ADBRL-2) 1

h. USAFSS

    (1) HEADQUARTERS
        (a) XR 1
        (b) CHO 1

    (2) SUBORDINATE UNITS
        (a) Eur Scty Rgn(OPD-P) . 1
        (b) 6940 Scty Wg(OOD) . . 1

i. AAC

    (1) HEADQUARTERS
        (a) ALDAA 1

j. USAFSO

    (1) HEADQUARTERS
        (a) COH 1

k. PACAF

    (1) HEADQUARTERS
        (a) DP 1
        (b) DI 1
        (c) DPL 2
        (d) CSH 1
        (e) DOTEC 5
        (f) DE 1
        (g) DM 1
        (h) DOTECH 1

    (2) AIR FORCES
        (a) 5AF(DOPP) 1
        (b) Det 8, ASD(DOASD) . . 1
        (c) 7AF
            1. DO 1
            2. DIXA 1
            3. DPL 1
            4. TACC 1
            5. DOAC 2
        (d) 13AF
            1. CSH 1
            2. DPL 1
        (e) 7/13AF(CHECO) 1

    (3) AIR DIVISIONS
        (a) 313AD(DOI) 1
        (b) 314AD(DOP) 2
        (c) 327AD
            1. DO 1
            2. DI 1
        (d) 834AD(DO) 2

(4) WINGS
    (a) 8TFW(DCOA). 1
    (b) 12TFW(DCOI) 1
    (c) 35TFW(DCOI) 1
    (d) 56SOW(WHD). 1
    (e) 347TFW(DCOOT) 1
    (f) 355TFW(DCOC). 1
    (g) 366TFW(DCO) 1
    (h) 388TFW(DCO) 1
    (i) 405TFW(DCOA). 1
    (j) 432TRW(DCOI). 1
    (k) 460TRW(DCOI). 1
    (l) 475TFW(DCO) 1
    (m) 1st Test Sq(A). 1

(5) OTHER UNITS
    (a) Task Force ALPHA(DXI) . . . 1
    (b) 504TASG(DO) 1
    (c) Air Force Advisory Gp . . . 1

. USAFE

(1) HEADQUARTERS
    (a) ODC/OA. 1
    (b) ODC/OTAO. 1
    (c) OOT 1
    (d) XDC 1

(2) AIR FORCES
    (a) 3AF(ODC). 2
    (b) 16AF(ODC) 2
    (c) 17AF
        1. OID. 1

(3) WINGS
    (a) 36TFW(DCOID). 1
    (b) 50TFW(DCO). 1
    (c) 66TRW(DCOIN-T). 1
    (d) 81TFW(DCOI) 1
    (e) 401TFW(DCOI). 1
    (f) 513TAW(OID) 1

(4) GROUPS
    (a) 497RTG(TRCD). 5

4. SEPARATE OPERATING AGENCIES

    a. ACIC(ACOMC). 2
    b. AFRES(AFRXPL). 2
    c. USAFA
       (1) CMT. 1
       (2) DFH. 1
    d. AU
       (1) ACSC-SA. 1
       (2) AUL(SE)-69-108 2
       (3) ASI(ASD-1) 1
       (4) ASI(ASHAF-A) 2
    e. AFAFC(EXH) 1

    f. Analytic Services, Inc. . 1

5. MILITARY DEPARTMENTS, UNIFIED AND SPECIFIED COMMANDS, AND JOINT STAFFS

    a. COMUSJAPAN. 1
    b. CINCPAC(SAG). 1
    c. CINCPAC(J301) 1
    d. CINCPACFLT(Code 321). 1
    e. COMUSKOREA(EUSA AGAC) 1
    f. COMUSMACTHAI. 1
    g. COMUSMACV(TSCO) 1
    h. COMUSTDC (J3) 1
    i. USCINCEUR (ECJB). 1
    j. USCINCSO (DCC). 1
    k. CINCLANT (0021) 1
    l. CHIEF, NAVAL OPERATIONS 1
    m. COMMANDANT, MARINE CORPS (HQMC) 1
    n. CINCONAD (CHSV-M) 1
    o. DEPARTMENT OF THE ARMY (TAGO) 1
    p. JOINT CHIEFS OF STAFF (J3RR&A) 1
    q. JSTPS 1
    r. SECRETARY OF DEFENSE (OASD/SA). 1
    s. USCINCMEAFSA (DPL). 1
    t. CINCSTRIKE (STRJ-3) 1
    u. CINCAL (HIST) 1
    v. MAAG-China/AF Section (MGAF-O). 1
    w. HQ ALLIED FORCES NORTHERN EUROPE (U.S. DOCUMENTS OFFICE). 1
    x. USMACV (MACJ031). 1

6. SCHOOLS

    a. Senior USAF Representative, National War College. 1
    b. Senior USAF Representative, Armed Forces Staff College. 1
    c. Senior USAF Rep, Industrial College of the Armed Forces 1
    d. Senior USAF Representative, Naval Amphibious School 1
    e. Senior USAF Rep, U.S. Marine Corps Education Center 1
    f. Senior USAF Representative, U.S. Naval War College. 1
    g. Senior USAF Representative, U.S. Army War College 1
    h. Senior USAF Rep, U.S. Army C&G Staff College. 1
    i. Senior USAF Representative, U.S. Army Infantry School 1
    j. Senior USAF Rep, U.S. Army JFK Center for Special Warfare 1
    k. Senior USAF Representative, U.S. Army Field Artillery School. . . . 1
    l. Senior USAF Representative, U.S. Liaison Office 1

7. SPECIAL

    a. Director, USAF Project RAND 1
    b. U.S. Air Attache, Vientiane 1

TABLE OF CONTENTS

		PAGE
CHAPTER I -	INTRODUCTION	1
CHAPTER II -	BACKGROUND TO PLANNING	5
CHAPTER III -	VNAF IMPROVEMENT AND MODERNIZATION PROGRAM PLANNING	9
	Summary of Phase II	20
CHAPTER IV -	TRAINING	22
	English Language Program	23
	Pilot and Support Training	25
	VNAF Air Training Center	27
	New Methods	28
CHAPTER V -	TACTICAL AIR CONTROL SYSTEM	33
	ALO/FAC Upgrading Plan	37
	I, II, and III Corps	40
	IV Corps	43
	Remaining Problems	47
	Summary	49
CHAPTER VI -	FIGHTERS	50
	Assimilation of F-5s	52
	A-37 Conversion	56
	VNAF and the A-1	58
	Weaknesses	60
CHAPTER VII -	HELICOPTERS	65
	Change of Mission	69
	Conversion to UH-1	71
	Phase II	73
CHAPTER VIII -	GUNSHIPS	78
CHAPTER IX -	AIRLIFT	84
CHAPTER X -	RECONNAISSANCE	91
CHAPTER XI -	FACILITIES	96

		PAGE
CHAPTER XII -	MATERIEL	100
CHAPTER XIII -	PSYCHOLOGICAL WARFARE OPERATIONS	108
CHAPTER XIV -	MANAGEMENT OF THE PROGRAM	112
CHAPTER XV -	PHASE III	115

FOOTNOTES

Chapter I	121
Chapter II	121
Chapter III	123
Chapter IV	125
Chapter V	127
Chapter VI	130
Chapter VII	132
Chapter VIII	134
Chapter IX	135
Chapter X	136
Chapter XI	137
Chapter XII	138
Chapter XIII	139
Chapter XIV	140
Chapter XV	140

APPENDIXES

I - VNAF Headquarters	141
II - VNAF Organizational Chart	142
III - Typical VNAF Air Division Organizational Chart	143
IV - Air Logistics Command	144
V - VNAF Beddown Locations	145
VI - VNAF Improvement and Modernization Plan	146
VII - Source of Phase I & II VNAF UE Aircraft	147
VIII - Composition of Vietnam Air Force	148
IX - Fixed-Wing Activations	150
X - Helicopter Activations	151
XI - Programmed Aircraft Buildup	152
XII - Summary of VNAF Forces	153
XIII - UE Aircraft Deliveries to VNAF, I&E Plan	155
XIV - Undergraduate, Transition, Other Training	156
XV - Defense Language Institute, English Language School	157
XVI - Pilot Training - VNAF	158
XVII - SVN Attack Sorties	159
XVIII - Sorties Flown	160
XIX - VNAF Personnel Status-By Grade	161

GLOSSARY 162

FIGURES*   Follows Page

1. Comdr, VNAF, Gen. Tran Van Minh 2
2. F-5 Pilot 6
3. VNAF and USAF Advisory Personnel 30
4. During I&M Program, VNAF Firemen Join USAF Units 32
5. U-17 Aircraft 38
6. F-5 - First Jet Fighter Appearing in VNAF Inventory 52
7. A-37-Most Widely used Jet Fighter in VNAF Inventory 56
8. Propellor-Driven A-1 58
9. Nguyen Cao Ky Led VNAF's First Raid over NVN in A-1s 58
10. VNAF Used One Squadron of H-34 Helicopters 68
11. VNAF Uses for C-47 84
12. ARVN Combat Troops Drop from VNAF C-119 86
13. U-6 Used in VNAF for Psywar, ARDF, and Liaison 94

* All Figures are UNCLASSIFIED.

CHAPTER I

INTRODUCTION

The new U.S. Air Force mission in the Republic of Vietnam was unmistakable and so was its priority. The Seventh Air Force Commander, Gen. George S. Brown, said in December 1969, "Vietnamization through enhancement of the RVNAF Improvement and Modernization program is a task equal in importance to the 7AF combat mission."[1] At the same time, a Senior USAF Advisor called the Vietnamization of the air war a "mammoth task,"[2] referring to the large-scale, many faceted, and highly technical training required to double the number of squadrons and men of the Vietnamese Air Force in three years. According to Gen. Creighton W. Abrams, Jr., Commander, U.S. Military Assistance Command, Vietnam, (COMUSMACV), "The toughest and longest training job we have with Vietnamization is the one the VNAF faces."[3]

Concern with the task facing the Vietnam Air Force (VNAF) and its advisors was offset by the professionalism of the VNAF. Its long combat experience was widely recognized and admired by USAF personnel in Vietnam. VNAF pilots easily transitioned into new aircraft types and learned new flying techniques. Once the VNAF took over a larger share of the air war, Brig. Gen. Kendall S. Young, Chief USAF Advisor, said, "Their successes bred pride, and that pride bred further successes."[4] But skill and experience would be diluted in the process of doubling the size of the VNAF, and the strain would come in the VNAF's weakest areas--management and logistics. In early 1970, advisory personnel and 7AF knew where some of these weaknesses lay. Teams from the Air Force Logistics Command (AFLC) helped the VNAF overhaul its materiel system, and VNAF squadrons were enlarged to make up for the shortage of middle-management officers. For the first time, the VNAF gave command attention to the management of flying hour rates, aircrew standardization, and maintenance schedules. As training programs expanded, new approaches were tested to meet the needs created by the Improvement and Modernization (I&M) Program. [5/]

The projected size and organization of the VNAF was determined not by the needs of the air war but by what size force was reasonably attainable with the time and resources available. The planners recognized that a reduction in total force levels in Vietnam would carry risks, and no one knew whether the enemy threat would decrease, whether the Free World redeployment would be modified, or the I&M Program prolonged in time and expanded in scope. [6/] Training was the major limiting factor and paced the program, because if the training program failed, many facets of the I&M Program would be in jeopardy. Initially, the USAF bore the major responsibility for VNAF training--much of it in the U.S.--and practically all training was in English. More and more, however, this training was shifted to Vietnam, and one major project was to integrate hundreds of VNAF trainees into USAF units. [7/]

The interdependence of the two air forces was also apparent in the overall planning for Vietnamization. The growing VNAF need for facilities and space on air bases required the redeployment of USAF units. The

Commander, Vietnam Air Force, General Tran Van Minh.
FIGURE 1

resulting joint planning committees filled the VNAF's need for long-range planning.[8/] Aircraft to double the VNAF inventory came almost entirely from USAF units in Vietnam, except for more than 300 helicopters furnished by the U.S. Army--for the VNAF, not the Army of Republic of Vietnam (ARVN), would provide helicopter support for ground troops.[9/] According to plans in early 1970, the VNAF would not assume certain USAF functions, such as interdiction of enemy supply routes outside of Vietnam, defoliation, B-52 bombing (ARC LIGHT), and possibly air defense.[10/]

Within the goals set, there was every indication that the VNAF would be successful in expanding and training its people to insure support of the Vietnamese Army. The VNAF would not be put to the real test until after 1971, but in the Mekong Delta area (IV Corps Tactical Zone) where the VNAF was already largely on its own, it proved itself to be up to the task.

CHAPTER II

BACKGROUND TO PLANNING

The French founded the VNAF in 1951 as a liaison flight. Manned by Vietnamese, it was part of the French Air Force under the command of French officers. In 1953, two observation squadrons manned by Vietnamese were added, but command, administration, and logistics support remained in French hands. The Vietnamese in French Air Force uniforms--at that time only a few hundred officers and airmen--were based at Nha Trang, with logistical support obtained from the main French depot at Hanoi.[1/] The departure of the French in 1955 left the VNAF with an inventory of aging Morane-Saulnier observation aircraft, Grumman F-8F Bearcats, and C-47s. The new VNAF staff organized these resources into two liaison squadrons, two fighter squadrons, a special-airlift-mission squadron, and a transport squadron.[2/] Throughout South Vietnam's first year of independence, the advisors to the VNAF were French.[3/]

In May 1956, a U.S. Military Assistance Advisory Group (MAAG) assumed responsibility for training the South Vietnamese Army and entered into a joint arrangement with the French to advise and train the Vietnamese Navy and Air Force. The Franco-American association lasted a year.[4/] At a time when unification of North and South Vietnam began to appear more and more impossible, the U.S. took action to expand the South Vietnamese armed forces. The French were not interested in aiding such an expansion and in 1956 left the U.S. with all advisory responsibilities. At that time, the French had trained only 92 pilots for the VNAF.[5/]

The next five years saw a remodeling of the force following the organization of the USAF, with English-language training and American management techniques. Expansion of the VNAF was still relatively modest. L-19s, T-6s, T-28s, A-1s, U-17s, H-19s, and H-34s replaced the older aircraft, and new facilities included a USAF-style depot, a major training center, a rudimentary Tactical Air-Control Center, as well as a total of five bases.[6/] By the beginning of 1962, the VNAF had grown to 5,700 officers and enlisted men and some 140 aircraft.[7/]

In November 1961, the USAF established a special unit at Bien Hoa VNAF AB to train Vietnamese pilots and maintenance personnel--Operation FARM GATE. Its objectives included "day and night tactical assignments; strikes against Viet Cong villages, marshaling areas, training centers, and resupply facilities; aerial drops; pre-strike and post-strike photo reconnaissance; and airlift."[8/] For nearly three years, there were joint operations under this program, with VNAF personnel required on each mission.[9/] As VNAF officers and airmen became familiar with USAF equipment and techniques from 1956 to 1961, the air effort became standardized, with more efficient aid possible under the Military Assistance Program (MAP). The period also laid the foundation for a much more extensive and accelerated expansion program over the next three years.[10/]

The decision of the U.S. Secretary of Defense in 1962 to support this rapid expansion was based on two urgent needs--first, to contain the growing communist threat to South Vietnam and second, to build a balanced air arm capable of supporting the Republic of Vietnam (RVN) army and its other armed forces.[11/] The USAF Advisory Group and the VNAF worked from 1962 to 1965 to diversify the roles and aircraft of the VNAF, further improve its organization, and expand its operational capability. The Advisory Group Commander, Brig. Gen. Albert W. Schinz, characterized the period as one of "explosive expansion of a very small air force into a fairly large one." The force grew from 5,600 men to 13,000 in slightly more than three years and from 7 to 16 squadrons and from 140 to 393 aircraft in the same period.[12/] In addition, to give the VNAF a more responsive chain of command, its wings and squadrons were completely restructured. A headquarters and one major operational base were established in each of the four corps zones in the RVN.[13/] Operation FARM GATE and a more capable Tactical Air-Control System expanded the VNAF operational capabilities.[14/] But by 1965, there were accompanying problems of maintenance, safety, overcrowded bases, and dangerously thin managerial resources at the middle levels.[15/]

The deployment of U.S. combat forces to Vietnam in 1965 had repercussions on all of the RVN's armed forces. For the VNAF, it brought a new phase characterized by greater emphasis on combat operations, for which the USAF also assumed an increasing responsibility. From 1966 to 1968, the VNAF acquired combat experience and consolidated gains from the previous three years. Six thousand personnel were added to its strength and the number of squadrons rose from 18 to 20. It was also a period of orderly equipment modernization and increasingly professional personnel.[16/]

F-5 Pilot - Veteran of nine years in the VNAF.
FIGURE 2

In 1966, the U.S. Secretary of Defense approved a modernization program, based for the first time on the concept of "self-sufficiency," which provided that when Allied air forces withdrew, the VNAF would be able to assume all air missions.[17/] Under the program, however, with its limited force structure and manning levels, the VNAF could not achieve self-sufficiency,[18/] as later modernization plans were to recognize. But the VNAF did make progress after 1965, and the Chief of the USAF Advisory Group from October 1966 to March 1968, Brig. Gen. Donavon F. Smith, could point to these VNAF achievements in his End-of-Tour Report:[19/]

> *"Above-standard flying accomplishments, particularly during VNAF reaction to the Tet aggression of January-February 1968.*
>
> *"Improved maintenance and demonstrated capability to acquire new aircraft systems without degrading overall maintenance performance.*
>
> *"Substantial progress in a force modernization/expansion program which will add six new types of aircraft and twelve squadrons to the VNAF inventory during FY 68-72.*
>
> *"An effective start toward resolving long-standing logistics problems.*
>
> *"Increasingly successful effort to match VNAF capability and performance to ARVN air support needs.*
>
> *"Marked improvement in VNAF training facilities, programs, and training accomplished.*
>
> *"Continued expansion of VNAF's ACW, communications, and related systems."*

By the end of 1968, the VNAF was making steady progress. One A-1 squadron converted to F-5s in April 1967;[20/] A-37s for the conversion of three other A-1 squadrons began to arrive; a transportation squadron converted to C-119s; and major construction and rehabilitation were carried out at most VNAF bases.[21/] VNAF capabilities and contribution to air operations were steadily growing. The really significant jump toward the goal of self-sufficiency was yet to come, although there was planning for it during 1968.

Apart from expansion, improvement, and modernization with which the 1968 (and later) planning would be concerned, certain weaknesses plagued the VNAF: lack of long-range planning, insufficient contact with the ARVN for the most effective use of close air support, need at all levels for firmer command and control, a high accident rate, poor logistics, and inadequate base support.[22/] In early 1970, all but the first of these weaknesses remained, in varying degrees.[23/] The basic situation, however, which the 1968 planning set out to correct, was an imbalance in the RVN armed forces. The End-of-Tour Report of General Smith's successor, Brig. Gen. Charles W. Carson, Jr., described this clearly:[24/]

> *"The development of a ground combat capability without a corollary development of the air support function is clearly exemplified in the RVNAF Improvement and Modernization Program. A large expansion of the ARVN began in 1967 while the VNAF force structure was maintained at the 20-squadron level. By the time the RVNAF I&M Program was implemented, the ARVN had almost achieved the force levels authorized. VNAF, on the other hand, with the longest lead-time training requirements, was just beginning a program that would not be completed until two years after achievement of the ARVN force goals. A 1967 program, which would have provided for a balanced increase in RVNAF combat capability, would have not only resulted in a more effective military force, but also would have achieved the goal at an earlier date than now possible."*

CHAPTER III

VNAF IMPROVEMENT AND MODERNIZATION PROGRAM PLANNING

The intensive planning phase for a true Vietnamization program began in early 1968 when the Deputy Secretary of Defense directed the Joint Chiefs of Staff (JCS) to develop plans for enlarging and modernizing the RVNAF "to the maximum extent feasible," so the burden of the war could gradually be shifted to them.[1/] He explained:

> *"There is urgency to accomplishing these objectives. In the course of negotiations, we may find it desirable to agree to mutual restriction on the military efforts of North Vietnam and the U.S. Accordingly, the structure of GVN forces must be reoriented to provide as soon as possible for self-sufficiency in logistics, airlift, and air and artillery support categories."*

He underscored that this would require "extraordinary actions" from all echelons.

In its planning, MACV used JCS guidelines passed down in April 1968 which specified: (1) an 801,000 manpower ceiling for the revised RVNAF final force structure, an increase of 84,000; and (2) "consideration of expedients which would enable the Vietnamese armed forces to take over the equipment of selected U.S. units which might be included in a schedule of mutual withdrawal." The guidelines considered this the optimum force that could successfully cope with any continued subversive internal aggression after U.S. withdrawal. In April 1968, Vietnamization of the war had not yet received general acceptance, and the Deputy Secretary recommended that "owing to political and psychological sensitivities, coordination with GVN/MJGS may be, at your discretion in coordination with the U.S. Ambassador, on the basis of strengthening RVNAF rather than self-sufficiency."[2/]

In May, MACV sent forward a proposed force structure for all of the RVN armed forces based on MACV's assessment of what the continuing communist threat to South Vietnam would be after mutual North Vietnam (NVN) and U.S. withdrawal. The principal assumptions were that the only North Vietnamese Army (NVA) personnel withdrawn would be those in clearly identified NVA units, with filler personnel left behind in VC units, and that the insurgency would get support from outside RVN. MACV strongly urged that matters of infiltration and the defense against outside aggression be dealt with in any overall planning for the era to follow hostilities.[3/]

The MACV force structure recommended that the VNAF build to 45 squadrons as follows: 17 helicopter, 7 liaison, 4 cargo, 4 gunship, 9 tactical fighter, 1 reconnaissance, and 1 training squadron; and for air defense, 2 squadrons of F-5s, 2 Hawk batteries, and 1 automatic-weapon MK-42 battery. Three of the existing A-1 squadrons were to convert to the A-37, and four of the H-34 helicopter squadrons to the UH-1. These conversions had already been planned under previous programs. This force structure was to be attained in five years, the limiting factor being the long lead time required to produce trained pilots and technicians.[4/]

This structure was described by MACV as not being "truly optimum," as there were limitations imposed by the availability of men, leadership potential, and "gross national capabilities." The deficiencies would have to be offset by U.S. support.[5]

When the JCS transmitted these proposals to the Office of the Secretary of Defense, the Deputy Secretary responded in June with further guidance for Vietnam's Improvement and Modernization Program, dividing it into two phases. The assumptions used in the May planning applied only to what would be called "Phase II"; further planning was directed for a "Phase I," which assumed continued U.S. participation in the war at the existing levels but with an expansion of RVN combat capacity to the maximum extent possible, especially in the ground forces.[6]

Rather than successive steps, Phases I and II were alternative plans providing options for varying developments.[7] But it was soon evident that the evolving situation could call first for Phase I and subsequently for Phase II. In fact, the Deputy Secretary directed the JCS to include a transition from one to the other in their planning.[8] Phase II planning, he added, should assume that most facilities then in use by U.S. forces would be available to the Republic of Vietnam Armed Forces (RVNAF), along with nearly all the U.S. equipment. A part of the planning should concern itself with the costs associated with Vietnamization--initial investment costs and recurring costs.[9]

COMUSMACV provided a recommended Phase I force structure to the Commander-in-Chief, Pacific Command (CINCPAC) and the JCS in late July 1968, based on the assumptions that U.S. participation in the war would remain the same and that the enemy threat would also remain. The major implication of the continued U.S. presence was that the Phase I planning did not need to provide a balanced RVNAF force, because inadequacies in certain functions, like helicopter aircraft, could be offset by American forces. MACV's proposal, for instance, considered only the need to expand the VNAF's helicopter force in IV Corps, where U.S. forces were small and where four UH-1 squadrons were proposed, along with a new wing organization. Elsewhere, the previously planned conversion of the H-34 squadrons to the UH-1 was to continue, one for one, with the number of aircraft in each increased from 20 to 31. Few other changes in the VNAF were required for the Phase I situation, except for moderate strength increases in air logistics, aircraft maintenance, base supply, and civil engineering to correct existing deficiencies and support the added units.[10/]

MACV pointed to a potential weakness in its Phase I development plan, which it considered "unavoidable in view of the guidance." This was the continued emphasis on expanding ARVN combat and combat-support elements at the expense of VNAF, Navy, and ARVN logistical elements which required long leadtime training. However, MACV intended to deal with this problem in its planning for Phase II.[11/]

In October 1968, Paul H. Nitze, Deputy Secretary of Defense gave the JCS authority for MACV to implement the Phase I plan, with minor field changes as required within the set ceilings. He said, "Please insure that the RVNAF are able to make maximum use of the combat strength without being hindered by inadequate logistic support"--an allusion to the weakness MACV had pointed up.[12]

In October, MACV submitted its proposed Phase II force structure of 40 squadrons, similar to the earlier nonphased plan: 14 helicopter, 9 fighter, 6 transport, 7 liaison, 2 gunship, 1 reconnaissance, and 1 training squadron.[13] In submitting this proposal, the MACV intelligence assumptions followed the general assumptions given by mutual NVA and U.S. withdrawal with residual NVA troops filling out VC units. MACV considered the RVNAF force structure in relation to the assumed threat. One of MACV's assumptions was that the VC would intensify terrorist and propaganda activities and would not conduct combat operations at a level exceeding regimental size. With 25,000 NVA fillers, the VC would try to maintain its forces at a strength level of 126 battalions, giving them the same relative posture they had before 1965.[14]

The plan allowed for flexibility. For the first year, FY 1969, the steps to be taken in Phases I and II were identical. After that, the decision to progress from Phase I to Phase II could be made at any time, and the schedule of either phase could be slowed down or accelerated, based on VNAF capabilities to assume new missions and variations in the enemy threat. An essential feature of MACV's proposal was periodic updating of the I&M Program. At any time, in either phase, shortcomings would be offset by U.S. units.[15]

As an order of priority, planners used the development of: (1) helicopter support for ground forces; (2) strike support for ground forces;

and (3) transport capability. MACV stated the "proposed force structure does not provide the desirable degree of self-sufficiency for VNAF, but it appears to be the maximum that can be achieved in a reasonable time frame (five years)."[16/] Availability of qualified personnel in the manpower base was the pacing factor, and MACV said that manpower possibly would not support an acceleration of Phase II.[17/]

The situation was sufficiently changed by November 1968 to enable COMUSMACV to recommend that "in view of recent developments...it appears prudent to go beyond Phase I and to move rapidly toward a Phase II posture. The Phase I plan is no longer consistent with the situation in South Vietnam....The Phase II structure is better suited to the present and anticipated conditions in SVN."[18/] Meetings and recommendations had already raised the strength level of the RVNAF from 815,000 to 855,600 and the VNAF from 21,000 to 32,600. General Abrams recommended a further increase of the RVNAF to 877,000, immediate implementation of Phase II, and a compression of the period during which Phase II would be carried out. The proposed VNAF strength at this time remained the same.[19/] CINCPAC agreed with COMUSMACV's recommendations and forwarded them to the JCS for approval and transmittal to the Secretary of Defense, Clark Clifford.[20/]

In December, Mr. Clifford took favorable note of General Abrams' proposal to accelerate Phase II and asked that a new, compressed schedule be prepared for the activation of RVNAF units, together with a plan for transferring necessary equipment from identified U.S. units. He also asked MACV for a plan to withdraw those U.S. units from RVN which would

"no longer be required or effective after transfer of their equipment."[21]
Henceforth, all steps in the RVNAF I&M Program were intimately linked to steps in the U.S. withdrawal from Vietnam.

Planning for this withdrawal was called "T-Day" planning, "T" standing for "termination of hostilities." In late 1968, MACV developed for CINCPAC five alternative time-phase T-Day planning concepts. One of these, Alternative D, provided for the residual presence of a MAAG, as did the other plans, plus a "shortfall package" which MACV described as:[22]

> *"A package tailored to make up specific shortfalls in RVNAF combat, combat support, and combat service support capabilities. The initial size of the shortfall package would depend on the actual time frame of U.S. withdrawal from RVN. The shortfall package would decrease as RVNAF combat, combat support, and combat service support units were activated in conformance with the Phase II goals of the RVNAF Improvement and Modernization Program."*

In December, MACV transmitted to CINCPAC an accelerated Phase II activation schedule, a list of equipment for the accelerated activations plans for transfer of necessary equipment from identified U.S. units, and plans for U.S. units which would no longer be required or effective after transfer of equipment. MACV plans for the VNAF called for all new units to be activated by December 1971, with turnover of equipment completed in 90 days. Helicopters were a major exception to the rule that U.S. units would turn over equipment to their RVN service counterparts; the U.S. Army was to transfer their helicopters to the Vietnam Air Force.[23]

The transferred aircraft were the O-1, A-37, A-1, AC-47, C-123,

CH-47, and UH-1. In the case of the UH-1, departing U.S. Army units could not provide enough helicopters for all the planned VNAF units to be activated, and MACV recommended that U.S. deliveries originally programmed for the Army be diverted to the VNAF. Direct MAP deliveries already scheduled for the VNAF in 1969 would provide the remaining UH-1s needed for the 13 squadrons.[24/]

To remove a major bottleneck in the Vietnamization program, the Secretary of Defense suggested that U.S. forces be used for training "quickly in Vietnam". In the VNAF especially, expansion was slowed by the necessity to give technical training to certain personnel in the U.S., requiring an extensive English language program which was costly and time-consuming.[25/] MACV recommended to the Secretary that Vietnamese forces be assimilated into American units in Vietnam in a large-scale, on-the-job training program:[26/]

> *"It is planned that the activation of the new helicopter squadrons will be accomplished through a method of infusion of personnel whereby VNAF and USARV /U.S. Army, Vietnam/ units are melded together. As the USARV units slowly phased out, VNAF would assume responsibility for the helicopters....The activation of fixed-wing squadrons would also be accomplished through the infusion method, and supporting equipment and supplies will be programmed through MASF /Military Assistance Service Funding/."*

Another method, discussed later in this report, was to train Vietnamese instructors in certain skills in the U.S., who would then organize classes in Vietnam. In May 1969, after a review of DOD programs, Secretary of Defense, Melvin R. Laird, said in a memorandum to the JCS and the Service Secretaries, "Vietnamizing the war should have the highest priority."[27]

At the Midway Conference of 8 June 1969 attended by President Richard M. Nixon and Nguyen Van Thieu, Secretaries William P. Rogers and Laird, Gen. Earle G. Wheeler, and other U.S. and RVN officials, the South Vietnamese leaders presented proposals for the RVNAF to be carried out in 1970 and 1971. Among them were the addition of F-4s, C-130s, and air defense missiles to the VNAF, and an increase of 170,000 men in the RVNAF strength ceiling.[28] Afterward, the JCS recommended only small increases, saying that "based on available manpower information, the GVN is rapidly approaching the upper limits of its manpower capability to sustain the present RVNAF force structure of 875,790. The force structure increase proposed by the GVN could exceed manpower resources."[29] Among the increases the JCS approved, however, was one for 3,200 airmen who would provide the greater logistical and base support needed for the VNAF's expansion to 40 squadrons.[30] On the subject of adding late-model aircraft, the JCS said to the OSD, "The types of equipment already being provided under the RVNAF Improvement and Modernization Program appear adequate in terms of current operational requirements and in terms of limited Vietnamese technical capabilities."[31] MACV had previously told the JCS: "No new sophisticated equipment should be introduced into RVNAF until there is an established capability to train personnel and maintain and operate the equipment, in addition to maintaining present equipment at a high state of operational readiness."[32]

In general, then, the JCS reacted skeptically to the GVN proposals at Midway, especially because they implied that the RVNAF, with further modification and expansion, would be capable of taking over major responsibility for fighting the VC/NVA at current threat levels. "This implication must be regarded with caution," they wrote to the Secretary of Defense. The I&M Program was designed for only a residual insurgency. They pointed out:[33]

> "...while the GVN proposal provides some additional offensive capability, the capability does not appear sufficient in and of itself, particularly in view of such problems as leadership and desertion, to enable the RVNAF to take over the major fighting responsibility against the current threat."

Despite these recommendations, Secretary of Defense, Melvin R. Laird, replied in August:[34]

> "Now the object of Vietnamization is to transfer progressively to the Republic of Vietnam greatly increased responsibility for all aspects of the war, assuming current levels of North Vietnamese Army and Viet Cong forces remain in the Republic of Vietnam, and assuming U.S. force redeployments continue.
>
> "Accordingly, I desire that the Joint Chiefs of Staff and Service Secretaries review the current RVNAF modernization and improvement program, and other on-going and planned actions to enhance RVNAF capabilities, with the goal of developing an RVNAF with the capability to cope successfully with the combined Viet Cong-North Vietnamese Army threat."

This memorandum was to culminate in a large-scale planning effort for "Phase III," described in a later section of this report. As far as its implications for the VNAF were concerned, it resulted in a combined 7AF-USAF Advisory Group Ad Hoc Committee comprised of all directorates and staff agencies of Seventh Air Force and all divisions of the Advisory Group which met daily for weeks.

The three phases of the RVNAF I&M Program thus reflected three possible developments in the war: Phase I, the war continues at the same level, the RVNAF are built up, and the U.S. forces remain; Phase II and Phase II Accelerated, the level of the war diminishes to the 1964-1965 level, the U.S. and NVA forces leave, the RVNAF are built up to cope with the residual insurgency; and Phase III, U.S. forces leave and the RVNAF are built up to a capability to cope with a continued NVA/VC threat at 1969 levels. In April 1970, Phase III had not yet been directed, although there were strong indications that a decision would be forthcoming.[35/] Except for some long leadtime training required for Phase III, only Phase II actions were authorized and being carried out.

This phase created a need for the VNAF to learn how to do its own planning. At first, because of the urgency to start recruiting and training, it was necessary to plunge into the program without a detailed prior plan, and the early planning had to be done by the Advisory Group concurrently with the first actions of the program. The documents published during this time were short and general in nature, primarily covering the conversion of helicopter, fighter, and gunship squadrons. During FY1970, however, the VNAF was gradually brought in, and more detailed joint planning began. To shift the burden to the VNAF and prepare them to develop an independent planning capacity, the Advisory Group helped the VNAF write a regulation in December 1969 which outlined how to prepare plans that clearly directed duties, responsibilities, and timetables. When VNAF plans written in the first half of 1970 are compared with their earlier efforts, the dramatic difference in scope, detail, and quality is apparent. By the end of April 1970, the Advisory Group's role in writing VNAF plans was reduced to simple monitoring and minor assistance. [36/]

The VNAF's progress is thrown into further relief when the immensity of the total planning effort is considered. In approximately eight months, the VNAF and AFGP produced 14 program plans covering the reorganization and mission of the VNAF, the activation of five air divisions and subordinate units, on-the-job training, proficiency training, self-sufficiency planning, helicopter augmentation, aircrew training, the activation of many units, and the reorganization of the Air Training Center, the Air Logistics Wing, and the Air Logistics Command. Equally important, during this time, the VNAF came to accept fully the value of effective detailed planning for good management. [37/]

Summary of Phase II

Phase II called for doubling the VNAF by the end of 1971--from 20 squadrons to 40 [38/] and from approximately 17,500 men to 36,000 men. The personnel strength was already doubled by January 1970, but most of the new men had to be brought to suitable levels of training before the squadrons could be activated. From an authorization of approximately 400 aircraft in January 1969, the inventory would grow to 934, fixed-wing and rotary.[39/] To achieve a command structure capable of controlling the expanded VNAF force, the structure based on wings would be changed by January 1971 to one based on air divisions.[40/] Some bases shared by the VNAF and the USAF would be turned over to the VNAF for its exclusive use and operation. In the Tactical Air Control System, the goal of Phase II was to upgrade the Forward Air Controllers (FACs), Air Liaison Officers (ALOs), and Direct Air Support Centers (DASCs), so they could control VNAF and USAF airstrikes in support of the ARVN.[41/] Although activation of all squadrons would be completed by December 1971, the Air Force Advisory Group expected another 9 to 12 months necessary before full operational readiness could be achieved.

CHAPTER IV

TRAINING

The success or failure of the I&M Program was dependent on the success of the training--the key to the later combat capability of the VNAF--and the key to training was knowledge of English. The program was like an inverted triangle with English language the tip at the bottom. Training was the pacing factor for timing the entire program.[1]

The training required by the I&M Program called for the largest single MAP-supported training program in USAF history: 15,000 personnel were in training at one time in early 1970.[2] The accelerated Phase II schedule provided for more than 1,400 pilots by FY 1972, almost all trained in the U.S. by the USAF and the U.S. Army (for helicopters). In addition, more than 6,000 maintenance personnel were scheduled for training in the U.S. and Vietnam.[3] As the Chief of the USAF Advisory Group said in August 1969, the acceleration posed problems of "tremendous magnitude" for the VNAF:[4]

> *"To accelerate the VNAF expansion program, as the U.S. Secretary of Defense directed, required that the highest priorities be established for personnel recruiting, English language training, CONUS pilot and technical training, equipment, and facilities. It also made imperative a reordering of priorities from a balanced progression of force development goals over a five-year period to a phased order of priorities emphasizing long leadtime requirements first."*

Training of the 15,000 men recruited during 1969 came first, and those destined for helicopter units were given the highest priority.[5]

Modernization of the VNAF, however, was kept as simple as possible to avoid delays and obstructions:6/

> *"Introduction of new, different, or highly sophisticated equipment, which would complicate the logistics structure and not contribute materially to RVNAF improvement, must be avoided in order to obtain the optimum use of the manpower resources allocated to the RVNAF."*

Vietnamization was a matter of teaching the Vietnam Air Force as quickly as possible how to perform tasks formerly done by a U.S. force of approximately 60,000 men and 1,200 aircraft, as well as those previously accomplished by USA rotor wing aviation and USMC/USN in-country air support.7/

English Language Program

The Vietnamese language has a limited vocabulary for the technology of aviation. Even when VNAF instructors conducted courses in Vietnamese, in many cases, they used English for the technical terms.8/ When faced with similar problems in their MAP programs, Korea, the Republic of China, and Japan had developed an English language program for students before they began flying and technical training in the U.S.9/ Instead of translating USAF technical manuals and technical orders into Vietnamese, the USAF decided to conduct the expanded I&M training in English.

In December 1968, the Advisory Group submitted Southeast Asia Operational Requirement (SEAOR) No. 181 to 7AF for a capability which would translate the English language into Vietnamese using a computer. The idea was to translate certain USAF technical orders for use by the VNAF when it became self-sufficient. The technical orders to be translated were identified, and in later 1969, AFSC was writing a program for a computer already located at 7AF headquarters. Late 1970 was the completion date planned for the SEAOR.[10]

The number of RVNAF personnel to be taught English under the I&M Program strained the existing resources. There were 2,500 students from Vietnam and 45 other countries who were graduated from the Defense Language Institute English Language School at Lackland AFB, Texas, but the Vietnamese I&M Program required almost 6,000 graduates in FY 1970 alone, exceeding the capacity. The U.S. Advisory Group at Tan Son Nhut therefore expanded the RVNAF English Language School system in Saigon and the English language programs at the VNAF Air Training Center.[11]

In March 1969, 7AF decided it could no longer supply English language instructors from its resources in RVN (one was required for every 10 students), and as a result, the Advisory Group obtained 386 instructors from the U.S. Most of these airmen taught in two off-base compounds in Saigon, where English language schools were established with a capacity of 160 classrooms. The others were sent to the VNAF Air Training Center at Nha Trang.[12]

During 1969, the results were disappointing. Although the washout rate for pilot cadets did not exceed the anticipated 20 percent, the rate for airmen was between 55 and 65 percent. Even the comprehension level of those airmen who were graduated proved to be lower than satisfactory when they were tested later in the U.S. Officials suggested several reasons.

Because of security-clearance investigations, there were long delays between the end of schooling in RVN and student departures for the U.S. The comprehension testing at Saigon was possibly compromised or the grades inflated, so students would appear better qualified than they actually were. In the case of some cadets, motivation was affected because they had been led to believe they were headed for fixed-wing pilot training, and found themselves in helicopter training instead. Another reason was related to the closeness of family ties in Vietnam. The students were apprehensive about leaving their families--although once in the U.S. their unhappiness gradually decreased. To alleviate this problem, a film was shown to the students before departure which presented a realistic picture of their life in America, the U.S. Armed Forces television channel was made available in VNAF quarters, and graduates from training in the U.S. gave lectures. The control procedures for English testing in RVN were strengthened to eliminate compromise. Where possible, the proficiency standards were lowered.[13] Most important, the number of students entering the Saigon and Nha Trang schools was increased to insure that quotas for the U.S. schools would be met. During the first half of 1970, 120 more language lab positions were installed in an air-conditioned, rehabilitated building at Nha Trang, more USAF language instructors were assigned, and the student capacity there was increased from 700 to 900.[14]

Pilot and Support Training

COMUSMACV assigned first priority in the I&M Program to helicopter training, second priority to fixed-wing training, and third priority to support training. [15]

The USAF Air Training Command and Tactical Air Command conducted all fixed-wing training in the U.S., except for O-1 pilot training which was the responsibility of the VNAF in RVN. Primary training for VNAF pilots was at Keesler AFB, Mississippi, where the students flew the T-28 and T-41 in a course lasting 44 weeks. After graduation, they trained at England AFB, Louisiana, in the A-37 and the C-47; at Williams AFB, Arizona, in the F-5; and at Lockbourne AFB, Ohio, in the C-119. They were then ready to be directly assigned to a VNAF operational unit in Vietnam. The O-1 liaison pilot training conducted in Vietnam at Nha Trang was preceded by a 12-week course in English to acquaint the cadets with technical and air traffic terms. [16]

The U.S. Army was responsible for all UH-1 helicopter training in a course lasting 32 weeks at Fort Wolters, Texas, Fort Rucker, Alabama, and at Hunter Air Field, Georgia. In primary training, the students flew a TH-55 or OH-23 light helicopter trainer and in advanced training, the UH-1. VNAF pilots transitioning from the H-34, however, were given their training in Vietnam. [17] Of the 327 VNAF cadets who arrived at Lackland for special terminology training in October 1969, and who should have proceeded to Fort Wolters to begin flying training before 31 December 1969, only 203 were able to do so on schedule. [18]

According to the AFGP Director of Training, about 2,000 spaces—helicopter mechanics and others—were lost in U.S. training schools because of English language deficiencies, placing the goals of the I&M

Program in jeopardy.[19/] Because of a similar problem with pilot trainees, a remedial language program was started at Lackland and Tan Son Nhut; 1,800 cadets were programmed into the helicopter program against an operational requirement of 1,500; and proficiency standards were lowered.[20/] But more important, the focus on training was shifted from the U.S. to Vietnam, especially for maintenance personnel.

Except for helicopters, maintenance and support training was primarily a USAF responsibility, although it was always planned to develop the VNAF's capacity to train its own maintenance and support men.[21/] Contract engineering technical service personnel and mobile training teams were sent to Vietnam to supplement programs at technical schools.[22/] Previously, USAF Mobile Training Teams had trained A-37 maintenance men when the A-1 squadrons converted to the A-37 and when AFLC reorganized the VNAF Air Logistics Wing.[23/] Beginning in February 1970, a 64-man team from the Air Training Command assisted 243 VNAF instructors specially trained in the U.S. to set up courses for mechanics and maintenance men at VNAF bases.[24/] More than 90 additional classrooms and labs were built for these instructors at Nha Trang, Tan Son Nhut, and Bien Hoa, RVN.[25/]

VNAF Air Training Center

The VNAF Air Training Center at Nha Trang AB was made up of six separate schools: a flying school, a language school, a communications and electronics school, a technical school, a general service school, and a military school. A seventh unit, the Air Ground Operations Course, trained air liaison officers and forward air controllers. In early 1970,

2,250 students were enrolled in these schools, and there were 1,050 more students at VNAF tactical wings, where courses were also taught.[26/] Military schools at the Air Training Center and other VNAF bases provided basic military training for cadets, NCOs, and airmen. The General Service School trained men in such functions as personnel, administration, air traffic control, and air police. An intermediate level Command and Staff College was established in January 1970 to improve VNAF middle level management; its first class of graduates totaled 39 captains and majors in March 1970. Its creation was a further step toward freeing the VNAF from dependency upon the USAF and in attaining self-sufficiency in management training for young officers and future commanders.[27/]

New Methods

At the beginning of 1970, the experience base of the VNAF was extremely narrow: 50 percent of the airmen had been in service less than 12 months and 77 percent of the officer corps were lieutenants,[28/] 25 percent of the captains and above were in training, and more than 58 percent of the enlisted men were in basic training or were unskilled.[29/] The airmen entered specialty training through a preliminary English language program, from which approximately 60 percent were washed out.[30/] The training program as originally conceived for U.S. facilities was overly ambitious. Schools in the U.S. were superior to those available in RVN, and it was necessary to get the I&M Program under way even though a final Unit Manning Document (UMD) had not been approved.[31/] The outcome of the training portion and the whole I&M Program was uncertain,[32/]

and new approaches were sought and tested to avoid slippages.

In general, the trend was to find solutions in Vietnam and reduce dependence on the U.S. facilities. The advantages were less cost, less time, higher morale, a reduction in English language needs, and greater self-sufficiency for the VNAF. The 243 VNAF instructors being trained in the U.S. were to set up 17 new maintenance courses at the Air Training Center, at Tan Son Nhut, and at Bien Hoa. About 2,300 students were programmed to graduate from the new courses during CY 1970. USAF mobile training teams would monitor the classes until the VNAF instructors demonstrated their ability to successfully train the students. [33/] At other bases, courses were being offered in 40 AFSCs--aircraft and weapon maintenance, general services, supply, civil engineering, and operational skills.

It was less simple to expand the in-country pilot training program which depended upon a significant decrease in hostilities and improved area security, according to an Air Force Advisory Group chief. [34/] Expecting that these conditions would improve, the Advisory Group developed a fixed-wing undergraduate pilot training program to be carried out at Nha Trang AB. This program was designed to provide enough liaison pilots for the three O-1 squadrons to be formed in the fourth quarter of FY 1971 and to continue to provide annual replacement pilots. Expansion of the Air Training Center, using T-41 aircraft, begun in early 1970 was completed by the end of April 1970. [35/] A rotary wing undergraduate pilot training program was also being studied in April with a view toward its establishment at Vung Tau AB. It would provide attrition replacements for the operational UH-1 and CH-47 squadrons.[36]

In the search for new approaches, the JCS suggested reducing the activity of combat squadrons, so they could be used for training activities, both flying and support. Headquarters 7AF responded: "Any reduction in VNAF squadron operations to permit their use in training activities would lower the combat capabilities of the squadrons or delay a squadron from becoming operationally ready."[37] In early 1970, there were no plans to implement the suggestion.

A successful innovation was the Integrated Training Program which allowed VNAF personnel to train on the job under 7AF personnel at bases where the two forces were collocated, at no cost to the MAP. When the VNAF airmen were brought to higher skill levels by the 7AF unit, they received 7AF certification, which was accepted by Hq VNAF.[38] Because of the collocation, complete integration of the VNAF men into the 7AF units was unnecessary, although this had been considered. Several working methods were to be used. Vietnamese who spoke English could be trained by Americans on a one-to-one basis, otherwise one translator was used for five trainees. In base-support functions, classes were conducted at the work sites by Vietnamese nationals. USAF and VNAF personnel operated certain facilities and systems jointly, until the day when the Vietnamese could operate them independently. In January 1970, integrated training, involving active participation of 7AF units as a specified part of their mission, included intelligence, photo-processing, civil engineering, air

Success of Vietnamization Program depends upon cooperation between VNAF and USAF advisory personnel.
FIGURE 3

traffic control, medicine, security and base defense, weather forecasting, and fire protection. Nine hundred VNAF personnel were in the program. Later it was to include more technical areas such as electronics and aircraft maintenance. Making better use of the Integrated Training Program was a large-scale supplement to formal training and to the VNAF's own OJT. 39/

Slightly different was a plan to integrate C-123 crews. Under Phase II of the I&M Program, three C-123K transport squadrons were scheduled for activation in the second quarter of FY 1972. The training schedules called for the VNAF aircrews to complete their combat crew training in the U.S. as early as one year before the activation. To prevent loss of proficiency, the Advisory Group and 7AF planned to integrate the crews into squadrons of the USAF 834th Air Division. Maintenance personnel would be similarly integrated as they became available. Ultimately, USAF personnel would withdraw and the unit would become wholly VNAF. 40/

Other actions and training techniques were studied in 1969. To train U.S. military recruits who had "limited aptitude," the Department of Defense developed special courses based on "Project 100,000" techniques which led to technical AFSCs. These training methods and materials relied less on verbal proficiency than on active participation by the student. Hq 7AF and AFGP thought the same techniques might be adapted to VNAF courses. 41/ In "functional context training," also favorably evaluated, the essential skills and knowledge in the task were isolated and taught directly without extensive theoretical training. 42/ The "PIMO" concept,

31

used by the USAF Systems Command after 1964, was also considered. This Presentation of Information for Maintenance and Operation system converted technical orders into new formats or "job guides," which used simple sentence structure, the nontechnical words actually used by working technicians, and limited information for each step in maintenance troubleshooting. The Hq 7AF Training Director wrote in his evaluation, "It has been applied successfully to the C-141 aircraft and could probably be adapted for VNAF use."[43/]

Summarizing, the limited availability of personnel, the need for extensive training, the low level of proficiency on the part of VNAF airmen, and the comparatively short time available for building the desired level of VNAF capability required the closest attention to the heart of the I&M Program--its training portion--to insure that unit activation schedules were met. If conventional methods faltered, unconventional approaches would have to be tried.

During I&M Program, VNAF firemen join USAF units for training.
FIGURE 4

CHAPTER V

TACTICAL AIR CONTROL SYSTEM

The VNAF would lack flexibility and independence after modernization if it did not have command and control of its own aircraft. Vietnamization of the TACS was stressed in Phase II of the I&M Program because of the intrinsic importance of a control system and because until early 1969, the VNAF's ALO and FAC program was weak.[1] Later that year, 7AF revised mission priorities and placed the training of VNAF personnel to take over the system above the mission of normal operations in the Direct Air Support Centers and Tactical Air Control Parties (TACPs).[2]

More specifically "as a matter of high priority," 7AF set out to upgrade the VNAF's capability to control all VNAF assets through the DASCs and to direct all VNAF airstrikes. Seventh Air Force planned further to increase training so the VNAF would also be able to control all U.S. airstrikes in support of the ARVN. An essential condition was to develop the VNAF Direct Air Request Net (DARN), so that all ARVN immediate air requests would be passed along rapidly. The goal was to turn over to the VNAF the responsibility for control of the TACS in each Corps Tactical Zone, (CTZ), enabling USAF personnel to resume an advisory role. The U.S. would retain responsibility only for B-52, herbicide, resupply, and other special missions.[3] These goals involved: (1) collocation of VNAF and USAF DASC and TACP teams to enable VNAF personnel to learn jobs better and eventually take them over; and (2) upgrading of VNAF FAC proficiency by 7AF FACs working with the Advisory Group. Again, for both tasks, it was necessary to start with programs to improve the English of VNAF personnel.⁴/

In all four corps zones, the obstacles to overcome were similar. With the expansion of the USAF role in the air war since 1965, the USAF had tended to assume responsibility on all levels for the control of tactical air activity. USAF personnel dominated the DASCs, the FAC program, and the TACPs of even the smallest ground units. VNAF personnel assigned to the same duties tended to be overshadowed, to work in their own corner, and to deal only with other Vietnamese personnel. As a result, they gained little knowledge of developing U.S. procedures and little in the way of self-confidence.⁵/

VNAF and ARVN policies contributed to this situation. The VNAF ALOs assigned to army units were generally young, inexperienced lieutenants. Because the VNAF used back-seat observers as FACs, nearly all ALOs were not pilots. For these observers to gain the confidence of the ARVN commanders and to function effectively as the commander's chief advisor in the use of tactical air was possibly too much to expect. In fact, experience showed that most of these ALOs were relatively ineffective. Even USAF ALOs often had a difficult time overcoming the reluctance of ARVN commanders to plan for proper air support of their field operations. The inexperienced VNAF observers assigned as ALOs were theoretically responsible for operational control over the more senior and experienced aircrews working in their area. The youth and inexperience of the ALOs and FACs and the relative lack of middle management in the wings was a result of the rapid expansion of the VNAF under the I&M Program, along with the relatively low priority the RVNAF gave the ALO program. Difficulties were compounded by the VNAF's organization of ALOs and FACs, which put them in different command lines. The most frequent VNAF explanation for the low quality of their TACP personnel was that experienced pilots had to be kept in the squadrons for combat duty.[6/]

Under these circumstances, VNAF officers considered the TACP a bad assignment compared to an operational squadron. VNAF officers were accustomed to better quarters and to living with their families, which was usually not possible at uncomfortable army posts in the field. Some VNAF officers believed housing also influenced the policy of having FACs operate from main bases rather than forward locations. VNAF officers explained that most pilots assigned to FAC duty were young and should be kept under the eyes of the older, more experienced pilots at wing headquarters.[7/] The policy resulted in less efficient visual reconnaissance because of greater distance, changing geographical areas, and less contact between the FAC observer and the army commanders.[8/] USAF Advisory Group officers said that VNAF FACs showed their immaturity in displays of poor judgment, like flying low and taking unnecessary risks, and in laxity in following prescribed procedures, such as keeping in radio contact and reporting promptly. USAF officers noted a decline in the proficiency of VNAF forward air observers following the long period in 1968 and 1969 when three A-1 squadrons converted to the A-37, with little combat activity for the observers.[9/]

Until November 1969 all VNAF FACs were observers, located in the

35

back seat behind the pilot. Only reluctantly did VNAF officials accept the USAF concept that one man could do both jobs more efficiently at a time when the military expansion program was putting a strain on manpower resources. The VNAF officers explained that two people were less likely to make a mistake; the observer had little else to do but his job--to reconnoiter visually, control strikes, and to assess battle damage. Advisory Group officers suggested that because VNAF Commander, General Minh, had come up from the ranks of the air observers, he retained a certain sentimental attachment for the function. The question was more than academic. With the manning problem in doubling the size of the VNAF, USAF advisors looked to the observers as a source of new pilots. Because observers had been recruited with the understanding that they were eligible to enter flight training and some were approaching the age limit, their morale was affected.[10/]

From a practical standpoint, it was difficult for an observer in the back seat of an O-1 to keep targets and strike aircraft in sight at all times, a problem that the pilot did not have to the same degree. In a two-man FAC team, the observer was constantly giving instructions to the pilot, causing time delays. A lone FAC could fly more reflexively and could keep his eyes and mind on both target and strike aircraft. On the other hand, U.S. FAC advisors agreed that in certain cases it was more desirable to have two men, as in visual search missions, in avoiding sensitive border areas, and in night flying. The observer could also relieve the pilot of minor duties like map reading. When the VNAF

Commander authorized one-man FACs in November 1969, he stipulated that some two-man crews be kept for working with U.S. aircraft. He believed that in addition to his other concerns in directing a strike, English was too much for a single FAC.[11]

But VNAF FACs, young as they were, did not do poor work. USAF advisors generally agreed that Vietnamese FACs and observers were bright and eager to learn, making good progress when the situation allowed. These FACs know "the country better than U.S. FACs will ever know it," according to the Advisory Group's Tactical Air Control System's specialist. But it was still desirable to have some U.S. FACs because of the need to speak better English or for airstrikes in support of U.S. troops.[12]

ALO/FAC Upgrading Plan

There were two categories of VNAF FACs: those trained and certified by the VNAF only and those trained and certified by the USAF. All combat ready observers were qualified to control VNAF airstrikes, but the emphasis in their training was in control of propellor-driven aircraft. The VNAF did not have the capability to train FACs for the control of U.S. fighter strikes.[13] But when the I&M Program determined to make the VNAF self-sufficient, there was a need to upgrade and certify VNAF FACs and ALOs by USAF standards, along with a similar program at the DASCs. The upgrading of FACs and ALOs was formalized by a MACV directive, a VNAF/7AF Operations Order, and a Joint VNAF/7AF/AFGP Plan for Upgrading VNAF TACS ALO/FAC TACPs, published in March 1969 and followed in May by the VNAF's own Plan Nr. 69-14.[14]

The joint plan called for three stages of training. During the first, the USAF ALOs at corps, division, and province levels developed the capacity of the VNAF ALOs to direct tactical air operations and to advise the ARVN commanders on air support of their troops.[15/] In many cases, the USAF ALO had never met his VNAF counterpart and in some cases, he had not even known there was one at the army unit headquarters.[16/] During the second stage, there was emphasis on training and certifying VNAF FACs by USAF standards. The third stage was to refine the first two training processes by allowing the VNAF to assume the ALO and FAC functions completely. There were no target dates but the turnover was to be as fast as possible.[17/] Other documents planned for a functioning and self-sufficient VNAF TACS by late 1970 or mid-1971.[18/]

The AF Advisory Teams in the field planned to monitor the program, but the burden of training was assumed by 7AF ALOs and FACs. The plan called for USAF and VNAF ALOs to work together closely, but collocation of the TACPs was not so much a goal as a condition for the attainment of the goal. After becoming proficient in the procedures, the VNAF ALOs passed all ARVN requests through the VNAF request net. They used only VNAF air, if available, and insured that VNAF strikes were controlled by VNAF FACs and that the After Action Report was sent to VNAF headquarters. At the same time, the U.S. ALOs worked to strengthen the VNAF working relations and prestige with the ARVN commanders.[19/]

In certifying English speaking VNAF FACs according to normal USAF criteria, the crucial prior skill, once again, was good English language proficiency. But once certified, they could direct all Free World strikes

I&M Program emphasizes training VNAF FACs, primarily in O-1. Less in use for FACing is this U-17.
FIGURE 5

to the satisfaction of the pilots and the ARVN commanders, in addition to having mastered the somewhat different techniques for directing their own growing jet force.[20] To eliminate the lack of prestige and experience among the ALOs and FACs, the VNAF stabilized their tours so that a minimum of ten qualified officers "of appropriate rank" was assigned as division ALOs to the ARVN. Where possible, the men spoke English and remained in the ALO/FAC system for one to two years; it was planned to reassign men only if there were other trained and experienced men to take their place.[21]

By early 1970, there had been substantial progress in the FAC and ALO upgrading program. Against an authorization of 152 crews on 31 March 1970, the O-1 "liaison squadrons" had 139 observers qualified as FACs for VNAF strikes and 140 combat ready pilots.[22] Forty-two pilots and 39 observers had also qualified as FACs for U.S. and Australian airstrikes, with 10 more in training.[23] From 505 sorties flown by VNAF FACs during January 1969, the number rose to 1,083 during December, a year later. During the same period, the percentage of all Free World FAC sorties flown by the VNAF increased from 10 percent to 26 percent.[24] VNAF FACs directed 72.2 percent of the VNAF strikes and 5.7 percent of the USAF tactical sorties flown (for a total of 31.6 percent of combined USAF and VNAF sorties) during the two week-period of 19 March to 1 April 1970.[25] By March 1970, the VNAF had manned and equipped all of the planned 66 Tactical Air Control Parties.[26] Almost all were collocated with their USAF counterparts and working with them,[27] although in many instances their effectiveness was still low.[28]

Limiting factors in the FAC and ALO upgrading plan were: (1) higher priority given to the VNAF helicopter program, affecting both the quantity and quality of FAC and ALO personnel; (2) slow rate of progress made by Vietnamese pilots, observers, and radio operators in improving their English; and (3) reduced number of sorties available for improving FAC proficiency. [29/]

The DASC goals were the same as for the TACPs: get counterparts together so that USAF procedures could be thoroughly learned and all operations turned over as rapidly as possible to the Vietnamese. As soon as the Vietnamese were ready, the key was to have them process their own requests for air support all the way. The U.S. processing, air support, and strike control were to be supplied only if the VNAF did not have the capability in a particular situation. In some Corps Tactical Zones, the VNAF DASC was geographically separate from that of the USAF's; in others, the staffs were located in the same DASC but worked in parallel and entirely separate fashion. [30/]

The progress made toward I&M goals in the DASCs can best be examined by corps zone since the conditions differed greatly from one zone to another. More detailed treatment is given to IV Corps because the conditions there allowed more rapid progress and provided an indication of what would probably take place in the other three zones.

I, II, and III Corps

In I Corps, the immediate goals in 1969 were the collocation of the U.S. Horn DASC with the VNAF's I DASC at Corps headquarters, the elimination of the USAF TACP associated with I DASC, and the reduction of DASC Victor to a TACP. The first of these goals was not met until April 1970. I DASC assumed responsibility for Horn DASC, which was to retain a backup role and handle special USAF missions which would not concern the VNAF.

The delay in meeting these 1969 goals in I Corps was caused by the fact that Horn DASC and DASC Victor were joint USAF-Marine operations, and Vietnamization could not proceed until April when MACV decided that the USAF would be responsible for the U.S. participation in the combined I DASC. The decision was related to the move of the U.S. Army XXIV Corps headquarters to the Horn DASC, when the Army assumed command of all ground forces in I Corps, including the Marines. The remaining USAF personnel in Horn DASC stayed to serve as an augmented TACP for this headquarters. DASC Victor was phased out in March.[31]

Between April and September 1969, all five USAF TACPs in I Corps were collocated with five VNAF TACPs. By September, the remaining three VNAF TACPs were visited periodically by a USAF ALO, and in addition the personnel from these three VNAF TACPs were rotated monthly among the collocated VNAF TACPs. The entire VNAF TACS was controlling all VNAF strikes, or an average of 55 VNAF and USAF strikes out of the average weekly total of 110 in I Corps--roughly 50 percent.[32] In fact, the 7AF Director of the TACC, Brig. Gen. John W. Roberts, expected the whole VNAF TACS to be self-sufficient by 1 July 1970. After a six-month period of further monitoring and phasing-down of the USAF elements, it was planned to turn over the complete system to the VNAF by the end of December 1970, except for special USAF missions and support of U.S. ground troops.[33]

41

In II Corps, the VNAF air control system in 1969 controlled only about 11 percent of the total VNAF and USAF strikes (44 out of a 400-per-week average)--the lowest of all four corps zones. Throughout most of that year, the USAF plan to upgrade the VNAF DASC proceeded according to schedule. By October, the U.S. DASC Alpha had taken over training responsibilities for the VNAF personnel working in II DASC at Pleiku. The USAF advisory contingent at Pleiku was increased from 4 to 12 people to handle the added control responsibility of U.S. airstrikes in II Corps in support of the ARVN.[34/] The added communications needed to work U.S. tactical aircraft could not be installed until March 1970 because of a delay in MACV's acquiring the additional microwave channels.[35/] Consolidation of DASC Alpha with II DASC, however, was not accomplished sooner, primarily because of the high level of battle activity during the early months of 1970. The commanders involved considered it an inopportune time to be carrying out fundamental command and control changes. On 15 March, after the battlefield had cooled, II DASC officially assumed all responsibility for II Corps, with DASC Alpha remaining in a backup status until mid-April when it reverted to an augmented TACP for the Commander of the First Field Force, Vietnam. At this time, not only the DASC but the whole TACS was placed in the hands of the VNAF, insofar as RVNAF forces were concerned.[36/] The VNAF personnel working in II DASC were expected to progress rapidly after the two DASCs were combined at Pleiku, for nearly all of them were strong in English. Ten of the 12 USAF TACPs supporting the ARVN had collocated with their VNAF counterparts by March 1970.[37/]

In III Corps, where there was only one DASC, at Bien Hoa, slightly more of the air control system was in Vietnamese hands by the end of 1969: the VNAF controlled around 22 percent of the total airstrikes (200 out of 900 sorties per week average). All of the 20 planned Vietnamese TACPs were operational and most of these were collocated with the American parties. Training of DASC personnel and ALOs was intensified; by the end of March, the VNAF controlled U.S. sorties in support of the ARVN, and it was planned to cut back the USAF element to a small advisory team by October. At this time, VNAF FACs were expected to be proficient enough to control 100 percent of the air for the ARVN.

IV Corps

IV Corps, however, presented a different stage of development in the Vietnamization of the air war. By March 1970, this corps zone was already nearly self-sufficient except for special USAF missions. The VNAF team in the DASC controlled all USAF, Australian, and VNAF airstrikes. VNAF FACs controlled 96 percent of all these strikes (an average of 437 out of 456 sorties per week). Collocation of the 19 TACPs was completed six months earlier, and the USAF had gradually withdrawn its personnel and equipment. And with 33, the zone had, by far, the greatest number of U.S.-certified FACs.[38/]

The advanced Vietnamization of air control in IV Corps was due to one fact: there were no parallel U.S.-GVN ground and air organizations. Almost all ground combat troops were ARVN. All tactical airpower based there were VNAF. This simpler situation was doubly interesting because it presented a rough analogy with what all of Vietnam would be like at the end of Phase II when U.S. forces were largely withdrawn from ground combat.

Until early 1969, the IV DASC operated much like the others. USAF personnel basically controlled USAF air, and VNAF personnel controlled VNAF air. Coordination, or even communication, was minimal. A CHECO report on IV Corps stated: [39]

> "On occasion a set of USAF fighters and their USAF FAC would arrive at a target at the same time as a set of VNAF fighters and their VNAF FAC. Both had been diverted by the DASC but neither side knew what the other had done."

But when an upgrading plan for DASCs was put into effect in early 1969, collocation was the first step, and it meant more than merely being in the same building. VNAF personnel worked alongside their USAF counterpart, and both USAF and VNAF communications were put into the same channels. Although there was great hesitancy at first, before long the VNAF officers were handling the majority of communications in English with the 7AF Tactical Air Control Center and all other parties. Forms and display boards were soon bilingual. [40]

This change was accompanied by a replacement of senior USAF personnel who had acquired their reflexes under the old system. According to the Chief of the Air Force Advisory Team to the 74th VNAF Tactical Wing: [41]

> *"The attitude of the USAF DASC supervisors earlier in this period was that the USAF was responsible for controlling airstrikes and that they could not take a chance on using VNAF resources....Their overall attitude was not cooperative....With the assignment of new USAF supervisors at IV DASC....the picture changed completely."*

A significant step taken during 1969 was to have the VNAF train all new personnel assigned to the DASC, which "immediately impressed on the new officer that the VNAF was in charge."[42/] By the beginning of 1970, the number of U.S. personnel in the DASC had been reduced from 30 to 12 and they served in a purely advisory role.[43/]

Out in the field, the problem for the U.S. Tactical Air Control Party personnel was one of educating and convincing the ARVN commanders that they should deal with the VNAF ALOs, who had in fact been in place for some time. The ALOs in IV Corps like those of the other three corps were young and carried little prestige. A fundamental problem of the ARVN was that the commanders did not routinely ask for tactical air before a sweep to soften up the area or at least to stand by. Often they asked for air support only after their troops had contacted the enemy. DASC logs for all of RVN show that although the ARVN was engaged in 50 percent of the combined US/RVN combat operations in 1969, only 35 percent of the attack sorties were flown in support of the ARVN.[44/] Moreover, the ARVN commanders had acquired the conviction that to get air support, it was necessary to work through the U.S. ALO, generally a major or a lieutenant colonel. At the same time the Vietnamese began to take over the DASC, the U.S. TACP diplomatically made known to the ARVN commander that if he wanted air support, he had to ask for it through his VNAF lieutenant ALO, "although not all the ARVN field commanders were pleased the arrangement." However, by early 1970, only one U.S. officer was left in each of the 19 TACPs, and he functioned only off-stage, as an advisor.[45/] The DARN net was completely in the hands of the VNAF everywhere in the corps zone.[46/]

In mid-summer of 1969, the 9th U.S. Infantry Division was redeployed from the Mekong Delta region, leaving little U.S. Army presence in IV Corps. This redeployment greatly simplified the program to upgrade the corps' VNAF FACs and gave the zone an early start in the I&M Program. Gradually, the primary mission of the USAF 22d Tactical Air Support Squadron (TASS) became that of training VNAF FACs. The squadron was so successful, it had worked itself out of a job by December 1969 and was transferred to Bien Hoa in III Corps (collocated with the 19th TASS), where it was to start a similar program. On 1 April 1969, IV DASC began fragging VNAF FACs to control USAF fighter strikes. The 9th ARVN Division area became the responsibility of VNAF FACs on 1 July, with all requests for air support processed by VNAF ALOs. The 7th ARVN Division area followed two months later.[47/]

The timetable called for complete transfer to the VNAF of operational responsibility for the IV Corps TACS before mid-1970, and it would have occurred sooner except for a shortage of O-1 aircraft needed for visual reconnaissance. In IV Corps, the USAF force had over 40 aircraft at its peak and about 50 percent of the flying was devoted to visual reconnaissance. Even with 10 more O-1s transferred from the USAF in January 1970 by the departing U.S. 22d TASS, the VNAF in IV Corps still had only 30. Furthermore, the U.S. Army had also been carrying a part of the reconnaissance role. It was expected that the total visual reconnaissance carried out in IV Corps would be reduced as a result of Vietnamization. [48/]

Remaining Problems

The problem of night forward air controlling also remained unresolved as of March 1970. VNAF FACs had not flown night operational missions since the 1968 TET offensive. The principal problems were a lack of suitable aircraft [49/] and the lack of night instrument training on the part of VNAF pilots generally. [50/] In January 1970, the Air Force Advisory Group officially urged the VNAF to develop a night capability for FACs as well as for fighters and gunships. To the USAF, the reasons were clear. Ten percent of all USAF sorties in Vietnam had been at night--against the enemy's movement of troops and supplies, and the night indirect-fire attacks on outposts and fire-support bases. [51/]

The VNAF's position in reaction to these urgings was that as of early 1970 they had no aircraft for night forward air controlling, nor were they programmed to receive any under the VNAF I&M Program. A SEAOR had been submitted, and until action was taken, VNAF headquarters was not inclined to make detailed plans for night FACing. The Advisory Group discussed what it considered a serious gap in the VNAF's capabilities, and even before the SEAOR was acted upon, U.S. advisors preferred to see some stopgap measure.[52/] The USAF aircraft which controlled night strikes in SEA were specially modified and equipped C-130s, C-123s, O-2s, OV-10s, and A-1s. And while most of these aircraft could not be included in the I&M additions to the VNAF inventory, the Advisory Group considered modifying some of the U-17s owned by the VNAF and acquiring more O-1s with improved instrument panel lighting. USAF FACs had been using the O-2A with a Starlight Scope. The AFGP Director of Operations believed that the VNAF needed an aircraft with "Identification, Friend or Foe" (IFF) equipment, UHF and FM command radios, flares, rockets, and preferably with tactical air navigation (TACAN). He suggested that the U-17 could be modified to use this type of equipment.[53/] By March 1970, in the middle of doubling its size, the VNAF had not yet dealt with the problem of controlling airstrikes at night.

The equipment installed on the VNAF O-1s used for daylight FACs also presented deficiencies. The radios were carried as "obsolescent and inadequate for FAC work" on AFGP reports in early 1970. "The lack of good radio communications," one report said, "degrades the capability of the FAC to control the strike aircraft and of the TACP to control the FAC." SEAOR Nr. 138 to install modern UHF and VHF-FM radios had been pending since 1967. By March 1970, it had been approved but not yet funded.[54] Similarly, the armament on the O-1 FAC aircraft was deficient as of December 1969. An AFGP 1969 End-of-Year Report stated:[55]

> *"Many of the USAF O-1E/G aircraft transferred to the VNAF were delivered without wing racks. Aircraft transferred in June and July 1969 are still without a rocket-firing capability. Although requests for modifying the O-1A from a 4-rocket to an 8-rocket configuration were initiated many months ago, no significant results have occurred. O-1s without rockets are nearly unusable for strike control, and with jet aircraft four rockets are sufficient for only one, or at most two, flights of fighters."*

Summary

It appeared the Vietnamese Air Force would be self-sufficient in the control of tactical airstrikes long before the end of Phase II. This meant the VNAF would be controlling all its air assets through the DASCs, operating the DARN, and processing all air requests, maintaining operational TACPs, and forward air controlling for all air support of the ARVN. By March 1970, the IV Corps DASC had largely been turned over to the VNAF. The III Corps DASC teams had been collocated with I and II Corps DASCs to follow within months. Collocation of the TACPs was 100 percent completed in IV, III, and I Corps and 83 percent completed in II Corps. VNAF FACs controlled 79 percent of VNAF air support of the ARVN in I Corps, 80 percent in II Corps, 48 percent in III Corps, and 96 percent in IV Corps. These FACs were controlling virtually 100 percent of VNAF and USAF air in IV Corps by April. Final training in TACS was under way in all remaining areas, and the VNAF's self-sufficiency was dependent on the success of this training and its proficiency in English.

CHAPTER VI

FIGHTERS

Based on past experience, the flying and maintaining of fighter aircraft would give the VNAF less trouble than any other aspect of the Improvement and Modernization Program. USAF observers of the VNAF--advisors and other pilots--were full of praise for the skill and courage of VNAF fighter pilots. While this admiration centered mainly around the VNAF's accuracy in putting ordnance on target, it also extended to formation flying, esprit de corps, and concern for being on time--from arrival at mission briefings to time over target.[1/] The Chief of the Air Force Advisory Group, Brig. Gen. Kendall Young, said:[2/]

> *"Just watch them play tennis or soccer or any sport. They have such marvelous coordination and capacity to learn....The great strength of the current VNAF force is their extreme professionalism, operationally. They are simply amazing at delivering ordnance accurately--better than USAF units. But then, they have done a lot more of it."*

This experience was the key. There were some VNAF pilots who had flown more than 4,000 combat missions. As General Young said, "No fighter pilot in the world, that I know of, has ever flown that many combat missions."[3/]

But if the skill of its pilots was the VNAF's strong point, management of maintenance, flying hours, and materiel was its weak point and required attention and assistance from its USAF advisors. Factors which made management more difficult were the increased number and type of VNAF aircraft. In early 1970, the VNAF had one F-5, three A-37, and two A-1 squadrons. Under Phase II of the I&M Program, they would receive one more 18-plane A-37 squadron and two more A-1 squadrons in July-September 1971.[4/] The F-5 squadron and the three A-37 squadrons they had were the result of conversions from the A-1.[5/]

Air Vice Marshal Nguyen Cao Ky, then Commander of the Vietnamese Air Force, wanted jets for the VNAF soon after they were first employed by the USAF in Vietnam in late 1964. The U.S. acceded, first by making a small number of B-57s available and later by providing F-5s and A-37s to the VNAF under the MAP. In August 1965, selected VNAF pilots, navigators, and maintenance personnel began training in the B-57 at Clark AB in the Philippines. By the close of the year, four crews were combat ready and flying operational missions with the USAF B-57 unit at Da Nang. For the first time in its history, the VNAF had a jet aircraft capability--but the program was only a stop gap measure.[6/]

As early as 1965, the shortage of USAF, USN, and VNAF A-1 aircraft was a matter of concern for CINCPAC. If other aircraft were substituted for the VNAF A-1s, they could be used to replace USN and USAF A-1s lost through attrition. For a number of years the armed services developed and evaluated aircraft designed to perform missions of the type the A-1 was then performing in RVN. Furthermore, capabilities of the A-1 were found to some degree in several other aircraft, among them the F-5, the YAT-37, and the OV-10A, but the relatively high unit cost of the OV-10A kept it out of the running for the VNAF.[7] To replace some of the VNAF's A-1s, then, CINCPAC suggested procurement of the F-5.[8]

Assimilation of F-5s

Conversion of VNAF A-1s to the F-5 required prior operational evaluation to assess the long-range implications. The USAF evaluated the F-5 in SEA in a project called SKOSHI TIGER from October 1965 to March 1966. Flying 2,651 combat sorties, a squadron of 12 F-5s was put through a variety of tactical air support missions under combat conditions. Although the emphasis was on close air support and interdiction, the evaluation also covered escort, combat air patrol, and armed reconnaissance.[9]

Originally designed with the MAP program in mind, the F-5 was characterized by simplicity and low cost. A lightweight, high-performance, supersonic, single-place, twin engine fighter, it was powered by two J-85-13 (upgraded) eight-stage, axial-flow turbojet engines with afterburners. There were two 20-mm cannons mounted internally and five stations were available for carrying various combinations of external stores. In addition, either two 50-gallon tip-tanks or two AIM-9B air-to-air missiles could be carried on the wing tips. Because of limited time, the plane had earlier been certified only for safety of flight, so that for the SKOSHI TIGER test, the 12 F-5s had to be modified.[10]

F-5 operational activity was divided into four distinct phases: in-country strike missions, interdiction missions, a phase designed to obtain the maximum number of sorties per day, and out-country ground strikes and

F-5 - First Jet Fighter appearing in Vietnam Air Force inventory.
FIGURE 6

escort. During in-country operations, the average bomb-load capacity was gradually and satisfactorily pushed up to 2,630 pounds. When carrying four M-117 bombs or their equivalent, the F-5's practical combat radius was found to be between 120 to 150 nautical miles (NMs), instead of the pretest computation of 230 NMs, and operating conditions in RVN further reduced the normal radius. Mission-planning factors, for instance, allowed for 10 minutes of combat with no allowance for loitering in the target area. Rendezvous and operation under the close control of FACs required additional high fuel-consumption time at low altitudes. F-5 mission-planning charts had allowed a normal fuel reserve of 600 pounds for approach and landing. This figure had to be increased to 1,000 lbs. at Bien Hoa AB where the VNAF later based their F-5s. Furthermore, the maximum cruising altitudes of heavily loaded F-5s were found to be lower than those shown by the performance charts, resulting in higher en route fuel consumption.[11]

In keeping with the VNAF's projected use of the aircraft, the primary role exercised in the F-5 evaluation was that of fighter-bomber, particularly in tactical air support where it proved to be effective. The F-5 demonstrated itself to be a versatile airplane able to match some of the better capabilities of other fighters. It was limited by its size but its simplicity made it easy to maintain. The F-5 airframe and general systems proved highly reliable. Most significant were the ability of the small, lightweight, honeycomb structure to withstand severe damage and the relative ease of repair compared with stressed-skin construction. In general, the F-5 appeared to be a useful aircraft for the VNAF short-range operations.[12]

The VNAF's 522d Tactical Squadron at Bien Hoa stood down in September 1966 to begin training for their conversion from A-1s to the F-5. Most pilots trained at Randolph AFB and Williams AFB in the U.S., with much of the maintenance training in Vietnam and at Clark AB. The crews returned from the U.S. and were operationally ready before the formal turn-over date of 1 June 67, but the maintenance program--the first jet-maintenance program for the VNAF--required the help of some 75 USAF jet mechanics for the first few months of combat sorties.[13] Meanwhile, the B-57s reverted to use by the USAF.[14]

The planned utilization rate was 35 hours a month with a desired in-commission rate of 75 percent.[15] These rates were not achieved until the following year, but after that time the VNAF F-5's maintenance situation remained solid. During 1969 the average utilization rate was 34 hours a month per aircraft (it would have been over 35 hours, except for 54 weather aborts),[16] but the in-commission rate was 85.2 percent. NORM and NORS rates for the year were 14.4 percent and 0.4 percent, compared with the 24 percent and 5 percent which were the USAF standards for the F-5. The F-5 gave the VNAF no problems with maintenance. From the standpoint of flying, the 522d Squadron did well in combat, despite the F-5's short radius of action, and most close-support missions could be completed. BDA figures from early 1970 were similar to the figures for the VNAF A-37s and the A-1s.[17] During the 1968 Tet offensive, the F-5 was used continuously. All the F-5 losses occurred on the ground. Six were damaged in two Tet rocket and mortar attacks on Bien Hoa AB, and the engine test cell was destroyed in a third attack.[18]

There were few problems encountered during the assimilation of the F-5 into the VNAF inventory. A tendency of the F-5 engines to stall was eliminated by an AFLC modification program at Bien Hoa in early 1968. Another problem related to the physiology of the Vietnamese pilots.[19] Apparently because of the humidity in Vietnam, the F-5 water separator was inadequate. Unless the heat in the cockpit was turned up to an uncomfortable level, the canopy fogged up at low altitudes, especially in the GCA pattern, on takeoff, and when diving below 4,000 feet for a bombrun. At times, water was sprayed back on the pilot. USAF pilots in the F-5 had put up with the discomfort, but the VNAF Surgeon General Dr. Giu believed that VNAF pilots could not withstand the loss of salt, because they drank less water than Americans, had a low-protein diet, and consequently tired more easily. By draining the separator more frequently, the problem was solved, and it recurred only on days when the relative humidity was unusually high. A similar problem was that, because of their shortness, VNAF pilots had to experiment with special thick pads on the seats and wooden blocks on the pedals. The problem of height was never considered serious enough, however, for the VNAF or the advisory Group to recommend a modification of any aircraft.[20]

A-37 Conversion

To evaluate the A-37A weapons system, TAC and PACAF conducted a program similar to the one for the F-5 from August to December 1967 at Bien Hoa AB, RVN. Project COMBAT DRAGON emphasized the four major functional areas of maintenance, operations, supply, and manpower. During the tests a squadron of 25 A-37s flew about 4,300 combat sorties, including close air support, escort, patrol, forward air control, armed reconnaissance, and interdiction.[21/] The results showed that the A-37A--developed from the T-37 basic jet trainer--was an effective strike aircraft in the South Vietnam environment and had limited capability in forward air control. Its principal tactical characteristics were excellent acceleration and deceleration, a very small profile, good maneuverability, modest loiter capability, medium speed, some visibility limitations, and a compact delivery envelope which provided excellent delivery accuracy. Versatile as well as substantial ordnance loads were delivered on targets within a 250-NM radius of the operating base. While flying 4,300 combat sorties, the aircraft sustained only 12 single-round hits. No aircraft were shot down.[22/]

The principal maintenance characteristic of the A-37A was simplicity of design. The good reliability of its systems and easy maintenance provided rapid turnaround. The aircraft also proved economical in terms of supplies, manpower, associated ground equipment, and facilities. Few maintenance man-hours were needed to produce a sortie. Finally, the low

A-37 - Most widely used Jet
Fighter in VNAF inventory.
FIGURE 7

personnel skill levels required to support A-37A operations further reflected the simplicity of the aircraft. These operational and maintenance characteristics designated it as an ideal jet aircraft for the VNAF. The JCS approved the A-37 for the three VNAF squadrons converting from A-1s as part of the MAP in RVN, except that the later B model instead of the A model used in the COMBAT DRAGON tests was chosen.[23/] The main difference between the A and the B was that the A-37Bs were stressed for six Gs, compared to five Gs for the A-37As.[24/]

Conversion of the three squadrons went as smoothly as the conversion to F-5s. One squadron at Nha Trang converted in late 1968; the two others at Da Nang and Binh Thuy converted in early 1969. All three became operationally ready before their programmed dates in mid-1969, despite late delivery of aircraft,[25/] and despite the fact that at Binh Thuy the wing was simultaneously converting two helicopter squadrons. As in the case of the F-5, there was a standdown period for each squadron during which the pilots received A-37 transition training in the U.S. and maintenance personnel were trained by a 36-man USAF Mobile Training Team. The Chief of the Advisory Group at the time said, "With minor exceptions, VNAF performance in accomplishing the three-squadron conversion was commendable."[26/]

Before their standdown, the pilots scheduled to fly the A-37 were sent to Bien Hoa. The VNAF pilots flew daily combat missions with the U.S. pilots, logging "stick time" on the way to and from target, though actual ordnance delivery was made only by U.S. pilots.[27/] New pilots were brought into the A-37 program by the VNAF at the time of the conversion, in addition to the pilots from the A-1 squadrons. The actual number of pilots trained was 162. Of these, 112 were A-1 pilots and the other 50, O-1 pilots who took T-28 training before transitioning to the A-37.[28/]

The VNAF pilots liked the A-37--for its long radius of action, loiter possibilities, the small size which made it hard to hit from the ground, the way it could hold a tight pattern, its ease of maintenance, and its ease of flying. In Vietnam, where the Free World Forces enjoyed air superiority, it was an excellent aircraft for VNAF preplanned strikes against enemy base camps, fortifications, and supply areas and for immediate strikes in direct support of troops in contact with the enemy.[29/] With these qualities, advisory personnel said the VNAF preferred the A-37 over the F-5, whose main defect was said to be shorter radius of action or loiter time--approximately 60 percent that of the A-37s.[30/]

Efforts in late 1969 and early 1970 brought the utilization rate up to the desired average of 40 hours a month for all VNAF A-37s, although until then it had consistently been below. On the other hand, as of January 1970, the VNAF had not been able to lower the NORS rate to an acceptable 5 percent--a situation which the Advisory Group brought to the attention of the VNAF Chief of Supply in December 1969.[31/]

VNAF and the A-1

When the three A-1 squadrons were converted to the A-37, some of the surplus A-1s were distributed as replacement aircraft to the remaining

Propellor-driven A-1 was for years the VNAF's only fighter.
FIGURE 8

Air Vice Marshal Nguyen Cao Ky personally led VNAF's first raid over North Vietnam in A-1s.
FIGURE 9

VNAF A-1 squadrons, afterwards regrouped as two squadrons at Bien Hoa.[32/] Two squadrons of A-1s were to be added to the force under the I&M Phase II, one at Pleiku and one at Da Nang. With one squadron of A-37s activated at Binh Thuy in the Delta, plans called for a post-Phase II total of nine fighter squadrons in the VNAF.[33/] Because of its age and the heavy use made of it in Vietnam, the A-1 required several modifications, but maintenance on the A-1 had become routine, and during 1969, it was consistently over its standard operational readiness (OR) rate and utilization rate. An inspect-and-repair-as-necessary (IRAN) line for the A-1 was put into operation at Bien Hoa in January 1970, completing the VNAF's capacity to handle all maintenance for the A-1.[34/]

It was in the A-1 that Air Vice Marshal Ky led the first VNAF multi-plane bombing attack on North Vietnam on 8 February 1965. Flying lead, Ky struck the military establishment of Vinh-Linh with six flights of four planes flown by the most experienced pilots in the VNAF. Although the sortie flew through heavy antiaircraft fire and every plane was hit at least once, 90 percent of the installation was reported as destroyed. Only one A-1 failed to return to Da Nang, the staging area for the raid. One lieutenant colonel bailed out over the South China Sea, but a helicopter rescued him. Ky himself was wounded. This daring and unexpected strike into enemy territory, occurring only five months after he had put down an army rebellion with his A-1s, made a dashing figure of Marshal Ky and contributed to the esprit de corps of the VNAF and to loyalty for its leader.[35/]

The performance of the VNAF was put to its severest test during the VC/NVA Tet offensive in January and February 1968. When the attack began on 30 January, 57 percent of the VNAF personnel were on leave with their families for the lunar new year. Enemy activity interfered with recall procedures, and the skeleton force on duty carried most of the load during the initial reaction. Within three days, 90 percent of the men were present for duty. 36/

Sixty-nine A-1s at Bien Hoa, Binh Thuy, Nha Trang, and Da Nang and 17 F-5s at Bien Hoa constituted the VNAF's strike capability at the time. On 31 January, they flew 368 missions. In all, 1,300 strike sorties were flown during the 17-day period ending 15 February: 30 percent for tactical air support, 57 percent for interdiction, and 13 percent for the escort of helicopters and truck convoys. BDA was 600 enemy killed and 1,000 military structures destroyed or damaged. Five A-1s were lost in the air and 10 on the ground in mortar and rocket attacks. The VNAF made a substantial contribution during Tet 68. The most meaningful indicator of its capability was a modest increase in the sortie rate. From a daily average of 65.5 strike sorties before Tet, the figure was brought up to 78, with little increase in maintenance capability. 37/ Such "surging" is relevant in discussions about the VNAF's ability to compensate for Allied withdrawals after completion of the I&M Program.

Weaknesses

Soft areas existed in both maintenance and flying-hour management, and USAF advisors were committed to pay the closest attention to them during the I&M Program.[38] General Abrams said in early 1970, "The VNAF has had management problems--for example, the limiting of the number of hours a man can fly--but they are learning and are overcoming them."[39]

Of the 7,215 strike sorties flown by USAF and VNAF fighter aircraft in February 1970, 40.8 percent were flown by the VNAF, despite the fact that the VNAF had only 24.6 percent of the USAF/VNAF aircraft. February was not unusual and preceding months show similar percentages.[40] Twelve months earlier with 17 percent of the total USAF/VNAF aircraft, the VNAF flew only 18 percent of the strike sorties.[41] The USAF Advisory Group's Deputy Director of Operations said in February 1970:[42]

> *"Despite imperfect maintenance management, the VNAF seldom fails to meet its sortie rates. And they aren't all that bad in management, all aspects of which incidentally they carry out by themselves now. For instance, they recently devised a good new system on their own for giving their fighters more flexibility. They stay on alert for two hours before taking off for a preplanned strike mission. If during those two hours no immediates come up, only then do they go. That way, they can also see how the weather shapes up. They are making progress in managing their assets. The weaknesses that remain are instrument flying, standardization evaluation, and getting good intelligence for fighter operations from Army G-2 and VR."*

The Advisory Group planned a program in March 1970 to develop a night capability by having the pilots devote a number of hours every month to instrument instruction. Most A-1 pilots rarely flew at night. Since the 1968 Tet offensive, the A-1s stood alert at Bien Hoa for any similar recurrence, but night missions were not scheduled.[43]

Similarly, in early 1970, the VNAF began to set up its own standardization-evaluation program, after frequent urgings from the Advisory Group. The VNAF was reluctant to take this action because of lack of suitable personnel, but it was finally convinced that the VNAF's growth to 40 squadrons would lead to a critical dilution of experience without an effective standardization-evaluation program for aircrews. In December 1969, representatives of all VNAF squadrons met at headquarters and were informed of a program that would soon produce manuals, regular visits to units, and standardization-evaluation officers for fighters, helicopters, transports, and liaison aircraft.[44/] The natural skill and coordination of VNAF pilots were not called into question. The AFGP's Deputy Director of Operations said, "You'll never hear a U.S. Air Force man bad-mouth the VNAF pilots. They have a healthy respect for them." When VNAF pilots were transitioning from A-1s to A-37s at England AFB, Louisiana, some of their USAF instructor pilots were embarrassed because the VNAF student's bombing accuracy was better than their own.[45/] But advisors were less sure what the expansion of the VNAF would do to this pool of fighter-pilot expertise. Some cited the decline of the German Luftwaffe when it was diluted during the latter years of World War II by an influx of new pilots. Others pointed to the job done by the U.S. Army Air Corps during the same period, with the same manning profile--large numbers of very young fighter pilots.

Past VNAF history gave one indicator. Accidents due to pilot error had always plagued the Vietnamese, perhaps because of the individualistic, "silk scarf" attitude they brought to flying fighter aircraft. In 1967, there was progress in lowering the accident rate, until the moderate expansion begun in 1966 diluted the VNAF experience to the point that 44 percent of its pilots had less than two years of flying and 23 percent less than one year. Accidents then rose to an all-time high in July and August 1967, with 61.2 percent due to pilot error, generally on takeoff and landing.[46/] Similar past performance tempered overly optimistic forecasts of the success for the I&M Program based solely on the skill and experience of VNAF pilots, for their ranks were to be thinned out by half with inexperienced, less-skilled young pilots. General Abrams said in March 1970, "The VNAF has made a good analysis of their quality and realize that it will decline as they continue to grow. They have programmed this in the system, so they will be able to lessen the impact of this quality decline as it comes."

The VNAF fighter force after Phase II would be diluted, smaller, as compared with the total 1969 Free World Force. By maintaining a sortie rate of 1.0 for each of its 168 fighters, it would be able to perform only 28 percent of the average Allied interdiction and close air support effort during the period of May to September 1969. By surging to a sortie rate of 1.5, this figure could be brought temporarily to 42 percent. If the Phase III fighter force proposed by 7AF were accepted, these figures would become 46 percent and 68 percent.[47/] On the other hand, it was possible that progress in pacification would reduce the VC/NVA level of activity so that by completion of the I&M Program, fewer sorties would be required than in 1969. The smaller, thinned-out fighter force of the VNAF was an example of what U.S. leaders referred to publicly as the risks inherent in Vietnamization.⁴⁸/

CHAPTER VII

HELICOPTERS

In the Republic of Vietnam Armed Forces, the Air Force--not the Army--provided air mobility for the ARVN's troops. Although helicopter squadrons responded to needs of the ground commander, they were not assigned to him. With so much of the RVNAF's organization a direct image of U.S. forces, the VNAF's helicopter squadrons presented a striking exception. As a USAF General said, "This was a decision made by the Ministry of Defense, but I suspect that it wasn't without Vice President Ky's influence." The Vice President was a former head of the VNAF.[1]

Before 1968, the H-34s owned by the VNAF were used almost exclusively for Special Air Warfare operations, but in January 1968, General William C. Westmoreland, MACV Commander, directed that the VNAF helicopter mission be oriented toward airmobile support of the ARVN. U.S. Army advisors in airmobile tactics were attached to the AF Advisory Teams. The AF Advisory Group prepared a training program designed to give the VNAF the capability to perform all the helicopter functions of an air assault mission, and in 1968, two H-34 squadrons in the IV Corps Zone were retrained. Their performance in combat was so effective, according to a former Advisory Group Chief, that it became a deciding factor in gaining approval for a plan to convert four of the five H-34 squadrons to UH-1s.[2] Using UH-1s earmarked for U.S. Army units in Vietnam, the conversion was carried out smoothly and efficiently in 1969, despite late delivery of aircraft.[3] The

65

conversion of these four squadrons marked the beginning of the VNAF's I&M program--the short-lived Phase I.

Phase II blocked out a much larger air assault role for the VNAF. In addition to keeping the one remaining H-34 squadron for unconventional warfare, the plan added eight more UH-1 squadrons and one CH-47 squadron. MACV directed that highest priority be assigned to activation of helicopter units, together with recruiting and training of pilots and technical personnel.[4/] The VNAF plan to implement the I&M Program said, "Especially focus on development of heliborne capabilities to increase the mobility of RVNAF combat units."[5/] The equipment for this portion of the accelerated expansion program was scheduled for tactical purposes, except that four were assigned to the Special Air Mission Squadron at Tan Son Nhut for liaison and transporting of dignitaries.[6/]

General Abrams, MACV Commander, reaffirmed that the principal use of new H-model UH-1 helicopters was to provide the ARVN with air mobility. The clarity of his language in a letter to the Chief of the RVN Joint General Staff leaves no doubt that, except for the four at Tan Son Nhut, he did not expect the VNAF to divert the helicopters to nontactical uses:[7/]

> *"I have been informed that the Joint Chiefs of Staff has approved my recent request to divert 60 UH-1 helicopters from their intended delivery to U.S. units to allow rapid conversion of four VNAF H-34 helicopter squadrons. This approval was based on my recommendation that these aircraft would be used primarily for ARVN air assault operations....The loss of these aircraft will be seriously felt by already understrength U.S. helicopter units, but I feel the need to improve RVNAF's airmobile capability is even more important....*

"I consider that the prime purpose of this helicopter force is for the support of ground forces in airmobile operations. Diversion of these critically important assets to activities other than support of the ground forces should be stringently avoided. Following is a list of priorities that I consider appropriate for these aircraft:

Priority I--Airmobile combat operations to include VNMC /Marine Corps/ and VNN /Navy/ combat operations.

Priority II--Medical evacuation.

Priority III--Supply and support of installations and operational units where water and land travel is impractical.

"I have made the decision to divert these resources to provide an airmobile capability for RVNAF which I believe is absolutely essential. I cannot stress too highly the necessity for their employment in a smoothly working relationship between the VNAF helicopter force and other service maneuver elements. Such a relationship is vital for success in RVNAF's expanding future role in this conflict. As you realize, the buildup of VNAF with UH-1 helicopters will decrease the capability of U.S. helicopter units. Therefore, I consider it essential that these VNAF squadrons are employed in the manner I have outlined above."

The purpose of creating a VNAF helicopter force, then, was to give the RVN Marine Corps, Navy, and primarily the ARVN an airmobile capability. But the Phase II end figure of 417 would not provide all the capability required. MACV had normally used as a planning factor two helicopter squadrons for each infantry division, giving air assault capability to one battalion within each of the divisions. This factor provided for transporting two rifle companies at one time, each company having an assault strength of 150 men. In addition, enough medium lift was required to support the assault with heavier equipment and supplies. Since the

UH-1 could lift 10 ARVN infantry men and since there were 20 slick--not specially configured--UH-1s per helicopter assault squadron, one and a half squadrons of UH-1s were required for each division, using the MACV factors.[8/] For medium lift helicopters such as the CH-47, MACV usually used a planning factor of one-half a squadron per assault battalion. Along with the UH-1s, this factor gave a total of two squadrons for the assault battalion of each division (1 1/2 UH-1 Sq + 1/2 CH-47 Sq). In addition, a UH-1 Squadron needed eight gunships and three command and control aircraft, making a total of 31 (20+8+3) UH-1s per squadron.[9/]

Using these factors, a total of 695 helicopters was required by the VNAF to carry out its stated mission for 12 infantry divisions: 31 UH-1s per squadron, 16 CH-47s per squadron, one squadron of 25 H-34s for special missions, and four UH-1s in the Special Air Mission Squadron. But at the end of Phase II of the I&M Program, the VNAF was scheduled to have only 417 helicopters: 12 squadrons of UH-1s, one squadron of 25 H-34s, one squadron of 16 CH-47s, and four UH-1s. Unless there were fewer infantry divisions than planned, a diminished need for combat asaults, or an increase in the number of helicopters under a later Phase III, there would be a continuing need for Free World helicopters to make up the difference, or a shortfall would exist unless different battlefield tactics were solved.

Furthermore, Phase II planning did not provide for the search and rescue of downed airmen or for medical evacuation from army battlefields by helicopters dedicated to these missions. It was thought that downed

VNAF used one squadron of H-34 helicopters stationed at Da Nang for unconventional warfare.
FIGURE 10

Vietnamese nationals were not as vulnerable as U.S. crew-members and that the assault helicopters were adequate for search and rescue, as well as for medical evacuation of ground troops.[10]

Change of Mission

Before examining plans for the substantial Phase II expansion of the VNAF helicopter force during FY 1971, it is instructive to review briefly the buildup through 1969. When in early 1968, General Westmoreland ordered a realignment of the VNAF's helicopter mission to give airmobile support to the ARVN, the force was comprised of five H-34 squadrons, two of which were moved to the IV Corps Zone. The training program carried out by the USAF Advisory Group with the help of U.S. Army advisors was not immediately successful, and the first airmobile operations brought criticism from U.S. Army units in the field.[11] Continued training by flying combat assault missions finally eliminated the criticism; in fact, the effectiveness in battle of the VNAF helicopter units based in the Delta was publicly recognized by the U.S. Army's 1st Aviation Brigade Commander.[12] In IV Corps during the last quarter of CY 1968, the two H-34 Squadrons completed 13,212 combat assault sorties, flew 4,131 hours, and airlifted 54,161 troops while taking part in airmobile operations with the U.S. Army.[13]

A major lesson learned during this period was that successful air assault operations could be conducted with the air assets including helicopters under the control of an air force rather than an army. The concepts and procedures employed by the VNAF were similar to those used by the U.S. Army when giving helilift support to its own troops. The VNAF made available to the corps commander a specified number of helicopters every day. The corps Tactical Operations Center (TOC) served as the planning center for air assault missions, and sorties were fragged by the Direct Air Support Center upon request from the Army's operations center. During the operation itself, VNAF "pathfinder" teams served as the communications link between the ground and airborne commanders, assuring that troop insertions into or extraction from helicopter landing zones were carried out as the ground tactical situation required.[14]

VNAF conduct of airmobile missions brought to the surface a difference in helicopter management philosophy between the U.S. Army and the Air Force. Army officers in IV Corps said the VNAF was less responsive to the requirements of Army commanders than Army helicopter companies were. They said that VNAF was management-oriented, in contrast to the U.S. Army which was user-oriented, and that the VNAF did not adapt easily to the need for unplanned surges.[15] However, both Army and AF helicopter advisors at VNAF headquarters agreed the difference in management techniques could be placed in a better perspective. The U.S. Army, they said, flew its helicopters hard, repaired them at night, and flew them the next day--if necessary, every day. Although this use often wore them out sooner, the Army simply sent them to a depot for rehabilitation or drew upon replacement aircraft.[16] The VNAF, on the other hand, as advised by the USAF, placed greater emphasis on maintenance management, because the VNAF would have fewer helicopters to begin with and fewer aircraft for replacements.

The USAF advisors stressed that flying-hour and maintenance management were necessary, and the Army helicopter advisor to Headquarters VNAF agreed.[17/] At all echelons and with all types of aircraft, the Air Force Advisory Group was emphasizing such management, as it was one of the VNAF's weak areas.

Allied officers in IV Corps noted that USAF officers in the DASC were hesitant to deal with helicopter operations because of their limited experience with helicopters and that VNAF officers sometimes followed their lead. The Advisory Group also noted that in 1969 and early 1970, RVNAF personnel in I and II Corps were not fragging enough helicopters for the combat assault role there. In March 1970, the U.S. Army Advisor attached to VNAF headquarters toured the northern bases and developed detailed fragging procedures which could improve the situation, if the ARVN cooperated. The advisor had found that much of the trouble came from the fact that the ARVN commanders preferred making their requests for helicopters to the U.S. Army rather than to the VNAF.[18/]

Conversion to UH-1

After its retraining for the airmobile mission in 1968, the VNAF's next major development in its helicopter program was conversion of four of its five H-34 squadrons to the UH-1, as part of the I&M Program's Phase I. This conversion took place between March and October 1969. All the necessary training was conducted in RVN, with the U.S. Army instructing a few VNAF instructor pilots from each squadron who in turn trained other pilots. Lasting 90 days, the Army's classes gave between 150 and 200 flying hours of training to 48 VNAF pilots. The remaining 117 pilots in the four squadrons were upgraded in their own squadrons by VNAF instructors and U.S. advisors. The syllabus consisted of basic transition to the UH-1, heavyweight missions, night formation, rescue, and combat assault. Flight engineers received their training at the VNAF Air Training Center, and USAF "Mobile Training Teams" backed up the army's schooling of flight mechanics by giving further on-the-job training. Integrated training of the entire crew, the last phase before the crews became combat-ready, was oriented to the assault mission, with many of the flights being made under combat conditions.[19]

Plans called for a USAF Mobile Training Team to train gunship crews in Vietnam for a period of 90 days in early 1970, after which the VNAF would be in a position to train its own. Only relatively experienced VNAF helicopter aircrews were to be assigned to the gunships. With the introduction of gunships and command and control aircraft to round them out in mid-1970, the squadrons would have all the necessary elements to perform their airmobile mission.[20] A major change planned for the gunships was to substitute the U.S. Air Force's XM-93 weapon subsystem for the U.S. Army's M-21. The advantages of the AF's combination of miniguns and rockets lay in its greater reliability with less maintenance, the ease with which in-flight stoppages could be cleared, greater accuracy, less weight, lower cost, and the greater ease with which the gunship could be converted into a personnel carrier. The XM-93 consisted of GAU 2B/A 7.62 pintle-mounted miniguns and two LAU-59 rocket-launchers. The rockets were fired by the pilot, while the miniguns could be fired by either the pilot in the forward mode or by the gunners in the flex mode.[21/]

One squadron in IV Corps, the 211th Helicopter Squadron, was the first VNAF unit to be equipped with the UH-1. It became operationally ready on 1 May 1969 and was soon providing twice as many aircraft and crews for combat missions as it had when equipped with the H-34. The squadron set a record in the VNAF for total and combat assault flying time and for numbers of ARVN troops hauled. In the annual competition, it was selected as the Best Combat Squadron in the VNAF.[22/]

Phase II

In late 1969, the AFGP Director of Operations expressed concern that activation in FY 1971 of Phase II's additional nine helicopter squadrons (8 UH-1 and 1 CH-47) would pose more of a challenge than the simple conversion of the four H-34 Squadrons to the UH-1.[23/] The concern was over the VNAF's capacity to provide a sufficient number of qualified aircraft commanders to meet the activation dates for the squadrons. The planned helicopter pilot training would provide each cadet with 210 hours total time; the VNAF required a total of 500 hours before upgrading to first pilot. The VNAF estimated that to gain the additional 300 hours it would take from four to six months of concentrated flying.[24/] With the active cooperation of the U.S. Army, the problem was solved in an unusual way. Plans called for training a nucleus of 220 VNAF helicopter pilots in the U.S., who would then integrate into U.S. Army helicopter units in Vietnam. After the new VNAF squadrons were activated, U.S. Army pilots and maintenance men would join them temporarily, along with the VNAF pilots, to help get the new units on their feet.[25]

The UH-1 Squadrons were scheduled for activation on the first of every month between 1 September 1970 and 1 March 1971, with the exception of 1 January 1971, when two would be activated. The CH-47 Squadron would be activated on 1 March 1971. In most cases, the VNAF units would be activated at the same base where Army helicopter companies were deactivating. Each Army UH-1 company had the same composition the VNAF squadron would have: 20 troop transports, 3 command and control aircraft, and 8 gunships, for a total of 31 aircraft. Only the H-model of the UH-1 would be given to the VNAF, and the squadrons would be activated with only 80 percent aircrew manning.[26]

Maintenance personnel started training in the U.S. in April 1969, and in October, VNAF cadets started basic pilot training at the U.S. Army Aviation School at Fort Wolters, Texas. By December 1969, the pilot and maintenance programs were behind schedule because of the students' troubles with English.

When they returned from the U.S., the nucleus of 220 graduated pilots was scheduled into the U.S. Army helicopter company in Vietnam corresponding to its new squadron, 90 days before activation. Then would begin three months of intensive training, the first part formal standardization, the second part operational flying. This flying would give practical experience under combat conditions, with the emphasis on airmobile operations. The Vietnamese pilot would have the same duties as the Army pilot, flying left seat or right seat on all missions, as conditions and progress allowed, with the Army pilot remaining responsible at all times as aircraft commander. The plan emphasized that the Vietnamese would not be excluded from any type of flying. The students were to fly six days a week, and Vietnamese holidays were not to be observed if there were a conflict with combat requirements of the day. During the three months, the Army units were to aim at giving each VNAF student 80-100 hours of flying each month until a total of about 250 hours was reached. Fourteen days before the activation date of the VNAF squadron, the Army unit was to standdown and prepare for transferring its assets. The actual transfer would take place during the two weeks following the activation date, during which time there was to be a minimum of flying.[27]

For the 90 days following activation, one Army operations officer, two instructor pilots, and 11 experienced aircraft commanders would be assigned to each VNAF squadron to assist with flight training. They would help, particularly with pilots previously trained in the United States who were not in the nucleus sent to the U.S. Army companies for 90 days, and who were scheduled for upgrading in the VNAF squadrons instead. The Army personnel would be carried as part of the Air Force Advisory Team for the area.[28]

As for maintenance training, VNAF personnel would be assigned to the U.S. Army units 60 days before their squadron's activation date (120 days before, in the case of the CH-47 Squadron). For 270 days after activation, about 45 U.S. Army and USAF maintenance personnel were to remain with each VNAF unit to supervise further on-the-job training, again under the control of the AF Advisory Team.[29/]

This helicopter augmentation plan was designed to give the RVN armed forces an airmobile capability by 1961 that would be adequate for the 1964/1965-level insurgency predicated by Phase II I&M planning.[30/]

The primary missions of the CH-47 medium-lift squadron were resupply, aircraft recovery, and movement of artillery. For these missions, the AF Advisory Group recommended in late 1969 that the squadron be equipped, not with the planned CH-47s, but with CH-53As.[31/]

The Advisory Group also recommended that the 219th Helicopter Squadron at Da Nang, still equipped with CH-34s, be converted to UH-1s. It was able to maintain its assigned aircraft strength only by drawing on an attrition pool created by the earlier conversion of the four H-34 squadrons to UH-1s.[32/] Maintenance was marginal throughout 1969. In October, the situation became so bad that the squadron stood down, partially for urgent and extensive maintenance. In December, unscheduled maintenance brought the NORM rate above 24 percent, and two more attrition helicopters were transferred from the pool.[33/] Owing to the danger of its Unconventional Warfare mission, the squadron lost 11 aircraft (through all causes) during the five months from May to September 1969. It had consistently exceeded its programmed flying hour utilization rate, and in September the Advisory Group notified the VNAF not to exceed 55 hours per aircraft per month.[34/]

The Advisory Group's Director of Operations made a matter of record his strong belief that activities of this squadron should be closely monitored, because of the sensitive nature of its mission and because of its dependence on an attrition pool of replacement aircraft. MACV replied to the group's recommendation for a conversion by saying it could not be acted upon in the near future.[35] In the meantime, the VNAF's Chief of Maintenance staff, working through the group, arranged for a reconditioning program for the H-34s in FY 1971 in a depot or by a contractor.[36]

CHAPTER VIII

GUNSHIPS

Some of the most encouraging results in the VNAF modernization program were produced by the VNAF's gunship squadron. Advisory personnel were unanimous in their favorable assessment of past experience and their optimistic view of the future of gunships in the VNAF. This praise was significant because gunship activity was expected to increase, while most other operational air activity would diminish or remain at the same level after the USAF activity was phased down. The gunships were to provide the primary support for an expanding Regional Forces/Popular Forces program.[1/]

The VNAF's first gunship squadron was composed of 16 AC-47s located at Tan Son Nhut AB. The squadron converted from C-47s in August 1969 after a delay of six months for late aircraft deliveries. As a transport unit, it was rated C-1 (fully operational ready) on 30 June 1969; on 31 July, it was rated C-2 as a gunship squadron. On 31 August, it was rated C-1 again, one month before the date specified in the conversion plan and without a standdown. While not standing down was not unusual for transition from C-47 to AC-47 aircraft, it did speak well for the operational training conducted prior to conversion in three AC-47 gunships, particularly in view of the fact that no USAF instructor pilot advisors were available after 1 April 1969. This first squadron was to be the VNAF's only gunship squadron until the end of 1971, when the second and last squadron, composed of AC-119Gs, was programmed to be added under the Phase II I&M Plan. 2/ For the second squadron, located at Da Nang and responsible for I and II Corps, the Tan Son Nhut squadron was programmed to train a nucleus of men in the AC-47 and send them to Da Nang. The transition to the AC-119 would take place there. 3/

"This squadron is better than any USAF AC-47 squadron that was ever over here," said a USAF Colonel whose duty was to evaluate the VNAF AC-47 unit. "When it comes to hitting the target, the Vietnamese can fly circles around us." He agreed that the explanation lay in the fact that the Vietnamese knew Vietnamese terrain, could see more on the ground, and had considerably more combat flying time than USAF aircrews. The average for the squadron in late 1969 was more than 6,000 hours, with several pilots having over 12,000 hours logged in the C-47. By comparison, USAF crews served a one-year tour and logged a maximum of 800 hours. Some VNAF pilots had been flying C-47s since 1958. The USAF Colonel commented, "It takes our people a while to become familiar with the terrain, the hamlets, the fields, and the forests--where one stops and the other starts. The Vietnamese seem to be able to acquire the target much faster at night." 4/

The training of crews in the first squadron was conducted mainly on fragged strike sorties in III and IV Corps. By the end of 1969, the VNAF "Fire Dragons," as the Vietnamese called them, were providing all of the gunship support for the IV Corps Zone. From sunset to sunrise, two or three of them flew airborne alert while six remained on ground alert at Binh Thuy and Tan Son Nhut. Through the IV and III DASCs, they were called in regularly for the usual gunship tasks of flaring for ground troops and fighter aircraft and providing aerial firepower for the defense of hamlets and outposts.[5]

Sometimes the VNAF gunships served as FACs for VNAF and USAF fighters and also for other gunships. When forward air controlling for USAF aircraft the biggest problem was the VNAF crews' limited English, but these crews believed they were underemployed and were eager to do more. In February 1970, their USAF advisors stated unequivocally that the VNAF AC-47 squadron could immediately provide essentially all the gunship support for III and IV Corps, largely relieving the USAF AC-119s of their remaining role in III Corps. There were no USAF AC-47s left in Vietnam in February 1970. "They have never failed to meet a target commitment," the Cheif Gunship Advisor said. "They could easily be used more than they are. And there have been no instances of Short Rounds, not flaring right, not meeting their time on target, or not firing accurately. If there had been, we would have heard about it."[6] Advisors to the 817th Tactical Squadron of the 33d Tactical Wing complained, on the contrary, that "it is the good stuff we never hear about." Frequently when they took a detailed look at logs and mission reports, they uncovered instances of outstanding work and resourcefulness which the VNAF people had never spoken about to their advisors.[7]

One typical example occurring on the night of 7 November 1969 came to light only because the USAF pilots involved telephoned the squadron's advisory team to relay thanks to the VNAF gunship crew. On that night,

80

Fire Dragon 03, commanded by Major Nguyen Sue Son, was on airborne alert over Tan Son Nhut AB when at 0310 hours, he was directed by the Tactical Air Control Center to proceed to Phuoc Thon hamlet. An ARVN unit there was being overrun by an estimated battalion of Viet Cong. Major Son established communications with the ARVN commander, who called for flares and fire support. Major Son laid a ring of minigun fire around the perimeter of the hamlet and then along a creek bed which was suspected to be the path that the VC were using to approach the hamlet.[8/]

Foreseeing that he would use most of his ammunition and flares before all the VC could be driven off, the major asked for more aircraft from the TACC, which then sent a USAF AC-47. Major Son learned, however, that the USAF Spooky gunship had no ARVN interpreter on board and that the ground troops had no American liaison or advisory people with them. With no FAC available in the area to guide the USAF Spooky, Major Son who spoke good English, decided to try FACing himself and directed the Spooky in its flare drops and firing until, like Major Son's plane, the Spooky was out of ammunition and flares.[9/]

The Fire Dragon's Commander then called for more help, and two UH-1 helicopter gunships were sent, which he also directed. Staying in the area, he acted as FAC for a USAF AC-119 which relieved the UH-1s. The attack was finally broken off by the VC, largely because of the VNAF AC-47 Commander's resourcefulness and capacity in serving as liaison, FAC, and interpreter for all air and ground elements, while he continued to pilot his aircraft.[10/] Such examples of VNAF pilots' understanding and prosecution of the air war were said to be far from rare. There was written testimony in the files of AFAT 1 of the respect the 817th earned from FACs and military units in its support of ARVN and U.S. Army outposts and mobile ground units, U.S. and Vietnamese Navy riverine forces, U.S. Army helicopter gunship sweep missions, and USAF tactical fighter strikes during the squadron's first six months of existence.[11/] The Chief of the USAF Advisory Group said by the end of 1969 this squadron's KBA figures were at least equal to those of a USAF gunship squadron.[12/] The VNAF was performing 28 percent of the total gunship effort in RVN. At the end of Phase II, with an increase in the sortie rate and the added squadron, VNAF gunships would still be handling only 80 percent of that effort. If the total requirement remained the same or increased because of greater support for Regional Forces and Popular Forces, there would be a "shortfall." If the requirement decreased when U.S. ground forces left, the two squadrons might be adequate.[13/]

A study of OR rates showed no problem was involved with VNAF maintenance of the AC-47. Providing pilots for the second squadron could prove to be a soft spot on the I&M Program, in terms of numbers as well as proficiency. At the same time that the Da Nang squadron was to be formed in late 1971, three squadrons of C-123s were also to be formed. Manning these squadrons with aircrews would require a minimum of 100 additional aircraft commanders, which could cause a serious problem as a result of the small number of transport pilots authorized at the end of 1969, and the stringent eligibility criteria for selection as candidates for aircraft commander upgrading. It would perhaps be necessary to divert considerable resources of a transport squadron (the 415th) from operational to training missions.[14/] There was continuing concern that multi-engine expertise would be diluted. USAF personnel thought highly of the VNAF's gunship capability and attributed the success largely to the experience level of the pilots. With the VNAF almost exactly doubled by the I&M Program, new recruits with no experience would dilute its ranks of experienced pilots. This dilution could occur in those areas of the VNAF's flying activities where, in the past, pilot experience had insured success and wide admiration. There is a clear danger in projecting past performance trends into the future and in trying to predict the results of the considerable and radical change that the I&M Plan would bring about in doubling the force. However, based on past experience alone, the VNAF gunship program up through February 1970 gave firm grounds for optimism.

CHAPTER IX

AIRLIFT

At the beginning of 1970, the Vietnamese Air Force had one 16 UE C-47 Airlift Squadron and one 16 UE C-119G Squadron, the result of an earlier conversion from the C-47. In FY 1972, three squadrons of C-123s were to be added under Phase II of the I&M Program.

It is likely that VNAF pilots logged more hours in the C-47 than in any other aircraft and certainly, the VNAF had more maintenance experience with it. The C-47 was diversely used. From April 1961 to July 1962, Vietnam's Vice President Nguyen Cao Ky, then an Air Force officer, personally led a series of night missions, using C-47s, to an area north of Hanoi close to the border of China. Single planes dropped teams of four special forces men trained in sabotage. Dropped with them were crates of ammunition, mines, weapons, radio sets, and food.

Each team had a specified assignment--to blow up highways and bridges, mine roads, ambush convoys, sabotage power plants. One team destroyed a large NCO training school. The C-47s also flew resupply missions to the teams as they exhausted their food and munitions. The teams eventually worked their way back to Pleiku via Laos along what was to be known as the Ho Chi Minh Trail. Lt. Col. Luu Kim Cuong, who was killed at Tan Son Nhut by a sniper during the 1968 Tet offensive, was a C-47 pilot and flew the first mission to the north with Ky. Before his death, he said, "We wanted to show the North Vietnamese that we could

VNAF uses for C-47 include: troop lift, cargo hauling, recon, and gunship.
FIGURE 11

infiltrate the North as they had the South."[1] Advisors cited the operation as a gauge of the VNAF's capacity and audacity and as an example of the wide use made by the VNAF of the C-47. The VNAF also used specially configured C-47s for reconnaissance, troop carriers, cargo craft, and gunships.

In early 1967, the VNAF 33d Wing at Tan Son Nhut had three C-47 transport squadrons, but in 1968 one was converted to AC-47 gunships and the other to C-119s. The C-119s gave the VNAF a capability to airlift cargo of greater weight and larger size.[2] In 1968 and 1969, maintenance on the C-47 was satisfactory, but there were continuing problems with C-119 maintenance.

Conversion of the 413th Squadron from C-47s to C-119Gs was technically completed in October 1968. Actual self-sufficiency was not achieved until after the withdrawal of C-119 pilot and maintenance advisors in FY 3/1969, according to the Advisory Team Chief attached to the 33d Wing. On 1 January 1969, the 33d Wing assumed responsibility from the Air Logistics Wing at Bien Hoa for the C-119's R-3350 engine buildup. Immediately thereafter, engine failures increased dramatically, with some failures occurring after as few as 60 or 70 hours of use. The OR rate during this period declined to a low of 50 percent. Advisors were finally successful in convincing the Wing's maintenance officer to service new engines properly before use and to take better care of engines on aircraft grounded for extended periods. In addition, the advisors put special emphasis on run up checks, engine conditioning and repair, and quality control checks to insure correct procedures. As a result, the average life for the R-3350 engine increased in the 33d Wing from 472 hours in FY 3/1969 to 609 in FY 4/1969 to 814 in FY 1/1970, above the USAF expected life of 600 hours. By October 1969, the OR rate rose to 73 percent, above C-1 requirements, and by 31 January 1970 it was 79.3 percent.[3/] The NORS rate, however, exceeded allowable standards from the start.[4/]

The C-119 Squadron had not yet attained a C-1 rating by March 1970, but this was primarily because of a shortage of aircraft commanders. The Advisory Team expected this problem would be overcome as soon as transition and upgrade training programs were completed. Despite crew shortages and maintenance trouble, however, the C-119 Squadron flew all its assigned missions.[5/]

One of the heaviest workloads borne by the VNAF transport squadrons was the receipt and distribution of air munitions for all VNAF wings (excluding common-use munitions, for which the ARVN had responsibility). Inspections uncovered major discrepancies in this area, principally in bomb stacking, separation of different types of ordnance, housekeeping, and facilities.[6/]

In January 1970, the VNAF transport squadrons were handling only two percent of all Free World airlift in Vietnam[7/] and only thirty percent of of the cargo for the Vietnamese Armed Forces.[8/] With the addition of the

ARVN combat troops drop from VNAF C-119.
FIGURE 12

C-123s in Phase II, the VNAF would be able to carry only ten percent of the Free World airlift in Vietnam, based on 1969 loads.[9] Since the RVN forces required less support than U.S. forces,[10] this capability might be enough, but either improved management to make the airlift more efficient or more aircraft in a Phase III might also be necessary. To increase efficiency of VNAF airlift, an Airlift Control Center (ALCC) and daily LOGAIR service to each VNAF base were started in 1968 and 1969. In January 1970, 7AF recommended that more aircraft be added to the airlift forces, especially C-7s.[11]

Before July 1968, VNAF airlift operations were conducted without benefit of a centralized management agency to coordinate airlift requirements throughout RVN. After a concerted AFGP effort, the VNAF established an ALCC which became operational two months later. During its first quarter of operation, the VNAF ALCC fragged 5,903 airlift sorties, moving 93,100 passengers and 2,286 tons of cargo in support of RVNAF forces. In 1969, following the success of the ALCC, the Advisory Group recommended establishment of an aerial port, but as of March 1970 no decision had been reached.[12]

In a move to help reduce the NORS rate, in October 1969 the advisory group proposed a daily LOGAIR service to each VNAF base. The plan called for a 60-day trial, but on 1 November, the VNAF Commander put the proposal into effect with no termination date. Using two C-119 aircraft, the daily scheduled service was "remarkably successful" in getting replacement parts to maintenance crews at the six major VNAF bases and helping to lower NORS rates.[13/]

The Special Air Mission Squadron (SAMS) at Tan Son Nhut was activated in July 1969, with a unit equipment (UE) authorization of four VC-47s, four UH-1s, and two U-17s, but for political reasons, the squadron was not organized as of 1 March 1970. No one at Wing level or in VNAF headquarters wanted to take responsibility for naming a commander and assigning the aircrews to a squadron which would work in such close contact with Vietnamese dignitaries. The sensitive problem was passed to the Joint General Staff, and in the meantime, missions were flown in the Wing's VD-47s by crews assigned to other squadrons. Advisory Group efforts to get the squadron organized were unsuccessful as of March 1970.[14/]

Turning to another subject which could ultimately affect the VNAF, a study of Air America's operations was conducted at Tan Son Nhut in December 1969 and January 1970 by an ad hoc group composed of representatives from MACV-CORDS, MACV 7AF, and the 834th Air Division. Among the group's recommendations was one to consider phasing down Air America in RVN and transferring the airlift role to Air Vietnam and the VNAF. Such action could create a need for additional transport during Phase III or after.[15/]

Another study in November 1969 explored the converse possibility of increasing the combat forces of the VNAF by contracting airlift and by converting certain military spaces in the airlift manning structure to civilian spaces. The Advisory Group found that 652 officer aircrew positions in the C-47, C-119, and C-123 Squadrons would thus become available. In the hypothetical conversion, these positions would be divided among the existing AC-47, AC-119K, A-1, and A-37 Squadrons.[16/]

As a result of an AFGP study, early in 1970 General Brown passed to the AF Chief of Staff, the recommendation that in place of the C-123s programmed for the VNAF under Phase II, a mix of C-130s and C-7s would be more advantageous. When Secretary of the Air Force, Dr. Robert C. Seamans, Jr., visited Vice President Ky in January 1970, the Vice President made a strong plea for one 16 UE Squadron each of C-130s and C-7s in lieu of the 48 C-123s. Ky claimed these aircraft would give the VNAF a greater airlift capacity with less of a drain on critically short aircrew resources.[17/]

The AFGP study used six criteria for comparing the C-123s to the C-130s and C-7s. It concluded that the latter two would give 8 percent more cargo airlift capability, 27 percent less troop airlift capability, 7 percent less operating cost, 20 percent fewer pilots, 7 percent fewer total personnel, and 23 percent less total flying-hour program. If the C-130 was approved for the VNAF, the 7AF Commander recommended the B-model of the C-130, because it had most of the features of the E and was more reliable than the A model. The greater range of the C-130E was considered unnecessary in the RVN. If the CSAF agreed with the recommended trade-off, the 7AF Commander, Gen. George S. Brown, was prepared to explore the proposal with MACV and the VNAF.[18/] But CSAF held to the C-123 because of the limited availability of C-130s.[19] In any case, a 7AF study completed in March 1970 indicated the C-123 offered greater returns in troop delivery capability, number of sorties, ability to use undeveloped runways, and tactical responsiveness.[20]

CHAPTER X

RECONNAISSANCE

At the beginning of 1970, the VNAF had a very limited reconnaissance function.[1] In the opinion of U.S. Advisors, the Phase II I&M Program would not provide the VNAF an adequate reconnaissance capability, especially at night or for Airborne Radio Direction Finding (ARDF).[2] The VNAF's capability in early 1970 was confined to the 716th Reconnaissance Squadron at Tan Son Nhut AB, which owned three C-47s with glass photo panels in the bottom of the fuselage, nine U-6As which flew psywar and ARDF missions, and one EC-47 which ran flight checks of navigation facilities in the RVN and performed no reconnaissance.[3]

Daily coastal surveillance from the Cambodian Border to the DMZ constituted 95 percent of the missions of the glass bottomed C-47s. For visual reconnaissance, the 716th Squadron furnished only the flight crew; Vietnamese Navy personnel did the observing. Earlier, the Viet Cong had used boats as a primary means of supply, but this was less true by 1969, due in part to regular VNAF coastal surveillance. The Vietnamese Navy men in the RC-47s had long experience with the fishing boats operating in the area. The aircraft flew at an altitude of 700 feet above the water, allowing the Navy men to observe each boat closely. As an Advisory Group officer said, "If there is one boat out of place, they can spot it immediately." When this occurred, they radioed to the crew of the nearest naval craft, who examined the boat more closely, often boarding and capturing it if suspicions were confirmed.[4]

In December 1969, a typical month, the three RC-47s flew 18 visual-reconnaissance sorties and 69 photo-recon missions. Through the three glass panels in the bottom of the aircraft, it was possible to take vertical, split-vertical (for stereo viewing), and oblique photos. Usually requested by the RVNAF Joint General Staff, 7AF, or MACV, all missions were preplanned and not the result of "immediate requests."[5]

The 716th Wing produced pinpoint, strip and mosaic photographs and did its own developing and printing but methods and equipment were outmoded. To improve the VNAF's capacity to process its photo work and deliver it more quickly, the I&M Program had originally included plans to construct a processing and interpreting building. A study conducted by the 7AF staff reassessed the feasibility of constructing a new facility at Tan Son Nhut to house the proposed VNAF Photo Exploitation Center. This study group recommended that a separate facility not be built. It proposed collocation of the VNAF Photo Processing/Exploitation operation within the 12th RITS facility. Approved by the 7AF Command element, officials were taking action to begin initial phase-in of VNAF photo processors into the 12th RITS operation in April 1970.[6]

With the planned addition of RF-5s to the inventory, it would be theoretically possible to perform the sort of quick tactical reconnaissance for ground commanders that would deliver the desired photographs to them within a matter of hours. The Joint 7AF/AFGP I&M Study Group in December

1969 took note of the fact, however, that the VNAF's 33d Wing at Tan Son Nhut had apparently no means of delivering their photographs to the requestors and did not attempt to do so: [7]

> *"Instead they box up their products, address them to requestor/users and deliver them to the USAF 12th RITS at TSN. The 12th RITS then gets the products to the users thru the most expeditious U.S. channels available at the time. Apparently, VNAF has no plan for delivery of recon products to user/requestors even after activation of their Photo Exploitation Center (PEC) and acquisition of the additional Phase II RF-5 capability. The 23d Wing at Bien Hoa (to which the 6 RF-5 aircraft are to be assigned) will have no organic photo processing exploitation element. Therefore, the VNAF concept is that the six RF-5s will deploy from and return to Bien Hoa. The exposed recon film will be downloaded at Bien Hoa and transported to Tan Son Nhut by the most expeditious means."*

The joint recommendation was that the VNAF should be encouraged to develop a program for delivery of its reconnaissance products to users. Since the 33d Wing at Tan Son Nhut had a transport squadron and a Special Air Mission Squadron, the delivery of these products could be made a mission of one of these squadrons. When vulnerability was not a factor, the UH-1 helicopters of the Special Air Mission Squadron "might represent an excellent delivery capability, since they could get the products to ARVN users/requestors at locations where fixed-wing aircraft could not land." The committee also recommended a study to determine if the gain in time achieved by recovering the RF-5s at Tan Son Nhut and unloading the film there would offset the possible operational and maintenance drawbacks.[8] Of the total photo reconnaissance for the Free World Forces in Vietnam in early 1970, only four percent was borne by the VNAF. Even at the end of

Phase II, with the addition of the six RF-5s, the VNAF would be in a position to carry only 10 percent of the effort. Recognizing the problem, AFGP, 7AF, and MACV later recommended that the Phase III force include nine RC-47s.[9]

Of the total amount of ARDF, the VNAF was responsible for only four percent. Phase II would bring no increase, although MACV considered it to be a critical mission and 7AF had specific recommendations on how to increase the VNAF's capability in ARDF.[10] By the end of 1969, the VNAF had flown ARDF for a number of years in U-6s--from two to four missions a day--all fragged and controlled by the Joint General Staff. Because of the classified nature of the mission and equipment, the 716th Squadron furnished nothing but the pilot, the aircraft, and maintenance of the airframe. The ARDF equipment was operated and maintained by personnel assigned from the Joint General Staff, who made their reports directly to the J-7 staff.[11]

It was assumed that after withdrawal of U.S. forces from Vietnam, the ARVN and VNAF would still need to locate the Communist forces with ARDF equipment. Because the areas to be covered were located throughout RVN, in the demilitarized zone, and along the Lao and Cambodian Borders, the existing VNAF fleet would be entirely inadequate.[12] The 7AF DCS/Intelligence recommended that more ARDF aircraft be added to the fleet and that a larger airframe be used by the VNAF. He suggested one squadron of 20 EC-47s (for the later Phase III), because this aircraft could take

U-6 used in VNAF for psywar, ARDF, and liaison.
FIGURE 13

improved ARDF equipment and reduce the total number of additional aircraft required to carry out all the missions once the USAF withdrew. A further reason was that the VNAF already had a good armament and electronics maintenance capability for the C-47. The training of all men necessary for operation and analysis could be done in two months--in Vietnam. The DCS/Intelligence further recommended that an ARDF-processing activity be established within the VNAF, as well as a control element accredited by the Joint General Staff, which would receive requests from tactical commanders, frag the aircraft, and report on ARDF findings. According to the recommendations, the ARDF would be grouped in a Tactical Electronics Warfare Squadron (TEWS) with forward detachments in all corps zones. [13/] As of March 1970, these recommendations had not been incorporated into any of the approved plans for the VNAF. The 7AF and AFGP said, "All [types of] missions being performed by USAF aircraft based in RVN can be performed by the VNAF with the possible exception of ARDF."[14/]

CHAPTER XI

FACILITIES

In 1969, it became apparent that the VNAF's I&M Program had to be linked tightly to the process of phasing down the 7AF. There were no longer separate, parallel programs; a step taken in one program usually called for a step in the other. At the urging of 7AF, MACV and PACAF recommended that the "T-Day Plans," which had been intended to govern the redeployment and deactivation of 7AF units, be scrapped and replaced by a new "integrated planning" concept that would coordinate both the buildup of the VNAF and the redeployment of the 7AF units. Higher headquarters approved the suggestion. The necessity for coordination was most apparent in the case of the transfer of aircraft and bases. Integrated planning also extended into VNAF training, personnel buildup, base support, joint planning, civil engineering, and construction. 1/

Joint planning by AFGP, 7AF, and VNAF allowed for flexibility in accommodating decisions regarding U.S. force reductions. It provided for incremental reductions leading to the turnover of bases to the VNAF or to their closure, while keeping a balanced VNAF/USAF combat capability as the redeployments occurred. The first step in this process was to survey the bases to be used by the VNAF to determine, by building number, which facilities would be needed by the VNAF, and at the same time determine what needed to be constructed by RED HORSE (the USAF construction organization) and the civilian contractors funded by the USAF and MAP. When a VNAF unit was due to activate or expand, the joint planners would insure that the USAF units occupying the needed facilities would vacate them by redeploying elsewhere in Vietnam or Thailand, to the U.S., or by deactivating.[2/] The bases surveyed by February 1970 were Da Nang, Pleiku, Bien Hoa, Binh Thuy, Soc Trang, and Tan Son Nhut.[3/] At Nha Trang, the major 7AF flying units had already been relocated to other 7AF bases before October. Only a transition force of about 800 USAF personnel remained (out of 4,000) to operate the base until the VNAF attained self-sufficiency in the skills of base support.[4/] In early 1970, the VNAF occupied six of these bases jointly with U.S. units. In addition to a base in each of the four corps zones, the VNAF would have Pleiku for forward deployments, Tan Son Nhut as headquarters, and Soc Trang as a spill-over base from Binh Thuy for helicopters in IV Corps. Soc Trang was added under the I&M Plan to accommodate the expanded VNAF force.[5/]

The next base to be turned over to the VNAF would be Binh Thuy, a turnover that started in January 1970 and was to be completed in early 1971. The same phased process for Pleiku was to take from January 1970 to early 1972. The VNAF operation there of six A-37s and eight UH-1s would grow to 105 aircraft by October 1971. The USAF strength of 2,500 at the end of 1969 was to be cut to fewer than 1,000 by July 1970. By the end of 1969, a USAF A-1 Squadron and the local rescue detachment had already moved.[6/]

After shrinking to a limited base operation, Tuy Hoa would eventually close. Bien Hoa would be turned over to the VNAF, except that an A-37

Squadron, a Tactical Air Support Squadron (TASS), base rescue, and the aerial port would remain temporarily as part of the transition force. Phu Cat would ultimately close, as well as Phan Rang, Vung Tau, and Cam Ranh Bay. When the final three squadrons of F-4s left, Da Nang would revert to the VNAF, and eventually so would Tan Son Nhut. Priority for reducing USAF forces went to those bases needed immediately by the VNAF I&M expansion, like Nha Trang, Binh Thuy, and Pleiku. 7/ Decisions and schedules concerning the other bases were to be determined later by what was decided at national levels. It was planned to turn over all the bases to the VNAF or close them, unless they were needed temporarily for the small USAF residual force. When the VNAF was completely self-sufficient, USAF forces in Vietnam would scale down to a MAAG.

The principal problems in the transfer of the bases were to come during the overlap period of dual occupancy, after the VNAF had begun to expand but before the existing USAF units had been relocated. In the cases where joint 7AF/AFGP/VNAF planning provided for the USAF units to leave soon enough, only minor construction would be required. In other cases, besides constructing facilities, Base Commanders and AF Advisory Team Chiefs were preparing to set up temporary accommodations and facilities, like tents, for the period of dual occupancy. 8/ In this regard, Da Nang presented the most difficult problems, of all, having always been highly congested. In March 1970, the joint planners were studying the possibility of moving the Army aviation company out, relocating the USAF units at other bases in Thailand and Vietnam, and arranging for the local U.S. contract construction firm to vacate its extensive facilities to establish a VNAF family housing area.[9]

At all bases, a common problem existed: the VNAF had acquired little capacity for handling base support. Before the I&M expansion, VNAF manning authorizations were limited to those spaces directly related to operating functions, and few skills were learned in the area of base support. At the time, it was an acceptable arrangement because 7AF jointly used the bases and provided base support to sustain combat operations. In planning for VNAF self-sufficiency, it was found that a great deal of effort would have to be devoted to developing these capabilities. In fact, the VNAF's lag in this area was one of the factors that limited expansion of the VNAF under the I&M Program.[10]

As it was, 7AF and the AFGP planned to devote a major portion of the VNAF training program to base-support skills and to leave a USAF augmentation group at each base until VNAF personnel were trained.[11] The only other possibilities were to have some of the training in base-support skills done by civilian contract, or to convert some of the base-support jobs to civilian slots. For the latter possibility, it was argued that available NCOs and officers could more efficiently be used as supervisors for the civilian force.[12]

CHAPTER XII

MATERIEL

The presence in Saigon of hundreds of small Renault taxis, of a model that had not been manufactured for 15 years was visual proof in early 1970 that the Vietnamese had high mechanical aptitude. They did as well with aircraft and modern jet engines. Pure mechanical ability, however, was not enough to insure a good materiel program. The VNAF had for a long time shown inadequacies in the areas of materiel management and organization--inadequacies that the VNAF, together with USAF agencies and advisors, were trying urgently to overcome before the doubling of the force put critical strains on the system.

As of January 1970, the operationally ready rate for VNAF aircraft compared favorably with that of the USAF, according to the U.S. Secretary of the Air Force.[1] However, as the 7AF DCS/Materiel wrote, "The logistics demands imposed by the rapid growth of the VNAF exceeded the capability of the Air Logistics Wing at Bien Hoa."[2] The VNAF's Plan 69-17 for the establishment of an Air Logistics Command commented, "The expansion and modernization of the ALW has not kept pace with the requirements to support the Improvement and Modernization Expansion Program. Thus, an accelerated effort is required."[3] Past methods were adequate for a 20-squadron force, but VNAF materiel could very easily become a soft spot in the expanded force. Brig. Gen. Kendall S. Young, Chief of the AF Advisory Group in 1969 and 1970, said:[4]

> *"Maintenance management, where you have a maintenance operational schedule for flying aircraft in a cyclic manner, scheduling aircraft by tail number into periodic inspections, making sure that your supply levels are constantly adjusted to take care of the demands--these are the kinds of sophisticated management skills the VNAF needs to be moving into. They need time-and-motion studies so that they can do things more efficiently in different ways....You see, up to now they have been concentrating on fighting as effectively as they can--kick the tire, light the fire, go off into the wild blue, and kill the Hun. They still have to do that, but in a more sophisticated and professional, a more managerial way....General Minh, the VNAF commander, recognizes this very well."*

In its earlier days, each squadron of the VNAF had a fair degree of autonomy and the headquarters had relatively little power. There was no logistics organization, each squadron coping almost independently with its own maintenance and supply problems. By 1966, however, the VNAF had established an organizational structure made up of wings which controlled the squadrons and were responsive to the headquarters. This new structure contained an Air Logistics Wing at Bien Hoa with an AFLC-style depot. [5]

The most far-reaching effect of the new structure was the consolidation of the shops and the concurrent introduction of specialized maintenance. Supply and repair became more efficient, but the Air Logistics Wing could not keep up with the rapid expansion. In the six years ending with 1968, the VNAF almost quadrupled the number of its aircraft and personnel. [6] The U.S. Military Assistance Program for the VNAF had increased from $15.3 million in 1965 to $264 million by 1967. During this expansion, however, emphasis was on the operational sector, and a simultaneous growth in maintenance personnel did not occur at the same rate. Furthermore, maintenance control centers had not been established.[7] The distribution of munitions was also a major problem, possibly because it was a responsibility, not of the VNAF, but of the ARVN. Access to the bases by road was often cut off by enemy activity, but early in 1970, when most roads were open in IV Corps, VNAF units still claimed the ARVN distribution system was not supplying airmunitions in needed quantities.[8]

In 1968, the USAF Chief of the Advisory Group who preceded Brig. Gen. Kendall S. Young said flatly, "Logistics is a major VNAF problem.... The VNAF's Air Logistics Wing is not yet capable of managing a logistics system or of providing effective supply and maintenance depot services." His group decided that the solution lay in sending logistics teams to Vietnam from the Air Force Logistics Command to bring depot operations up to a satisfactory level.[9] The first AFLC teams were successful, and others were requested for most aspects of logistics work. Team assistance was projected to continue throughout the balance of 1970,[10] and the 7AF DCS/Materiel said they would be necessary throughout all of Phase II.[11]

These teams were responsible for conducting wall-to-wall inventories, "purifying" stock records so that they reflected actual stocks on hand, computing requisite stock levels of supply items, rewarehousing, writing a logistics manual for the VNAF, disposing of excesses, surveying the VNAF logistics system, and drawing up a proposal for the complete reorganization of the logistics wing into an Air Logistics Command.[12] By the end of 1969, stock records were more accurate "than at any time during the past two years," according to the Advisory Group. The danger of this approach, recognized by advisory personnel, was that the AFLC teams, instead of assisting, would do the work themselves--which actually happened. The problem was compounded by a tendency on the part of the Vietnamese to lose enthusiasm for thos supply programs which they felt "left out of." Because of a shortage of VNAF supply people and the low skill level of those available, one of the Air Logistics Command's greatest needs in late 1969 was more training for its supply personnel. 13/

At the same time as the establishment of the Air Logistics Wing at Bien Hoa in 1965 and the later improvement in supply procedures, a depot-level maintenance and overhaul organization was developed at Bien Hoa, again with the aid of AFLC teams. By late 1969, as the Wing converted to the Air Logistics Command, the resemblance to an AFLC air materiel area was complete. Its maintenance directorate was organized around the functions of industrial engineering, aircraft and propulsion repair, fabrications, aircraft support, and quality and production control. The depot had a 100% repair capability for the O-1 and U-17 aircraft and could perform IRAN maintenance on the O-1. In January 1970, an AFLC team was preparing the depot to perform IRAN on A-1s. By June 1971, the depot was expected to perform IRAN and depot-level maintenance on the UH-1 helicopter--destined to become the VNAF's most common aircraft by the end of the I&M Program. Depot-level repair was available for the J-85 engine and was programmed for T-53 engines. Bien Hoa also had a newly constructed precision measuring equipment laboratory, as well as a building for the repair of 75 different types of communications and electronics equipment. 14/ If the

VNAF succeeded in running this supply and maintenance depot efficiently, it would indicate that VNAF logistics had at last come of age. In early 1970, however, it was too early to tell.

At the bases, advisory efforts to improve supply and field maintenance progressed during 1969. The most notable accomplishment was the building of J-85 engine test stands at Binh Thuy, Nha Trang, and Da Nang, which allowed further organic maintenance for the VNAF's A-37 jets. The F-5s at Bien Hoa used the depot there. 15/

In the typical VNAF wing organization, basic materiel functions were performed by a "technical group" responsible for the flight line, periodic and field maintenance, and supply. A wing supply squadron account supported 25-30,000 line items. Requisitions for items not in stock were mailed to the Air Logistics Command, unless they were items common to the ARVN--like certain ammunition, vehicle parts, and civil engineering supplies--in which case the requisitions were mailed to the ARVN tech services center. Support for the UH-1 helicopters came from a U.S. Army materiel center at Tan Son Nhut. 16/

Fuels were also a responsibility of the supply squadron, with all major bases stocking JP-4 and 115/145 fuel. But in early 1970, all delivery of aviation fuel was still under U.S. control and was delivered to the wing supply squadrons through U.S. supply channels. Munitions storage and loading was handled at VNAF bases by an armament and munitions squadron under the technical group. By late 1969, the VNAF had learned to maintain the armament systems on the AC-47, A-37, F-5, A-1, O-1, U-17, and UH-1 aircraft.[17]

Regarding overall aircraft maintenance, the old H-34 helicopter, the C-119G, and the A-37 were the only types which seemed consistently to give trouble. In the case of the C-119G, its NORS rate was excessive during 1969 and was expected to remain so for some time. The problem was poor parts management at depot level, compounded by the long time required to overhaul the engine in the U.S. Of the 154 parts requisitioned for the A-37 between 1 October and 19 December 1969, 63 had to be filled from a depot in the U.S., indicating that something was wrong with the stock levels maintained in Vietnam. The AF Advisory Group brought this situation to the attention of the VNAF Chief of Supply in December 1969.[18]

Throughout 1969, weapon system support logistics officers were assigned to Advisory Teams at the wings for specific aircraft. By September 1969, there were USAF supply and maintenance specialists for the F-5, H-34, A-37, and UH-1.[19] A problem at one wing may have been due to a difference in military traditions. The Chief of the Advisory Team at Tan Son Nhut found that Vietnamese maintenance and flight line officers were reluctant to discuss their problems with the USAF maintenance officer, a chief master sergeant, perhaps because the VNAF officers had been accustomed to the less-egalitarian French tradition.[20]

Another set of circumstances which could create problems was the maintenance of UH-1 helicopters. The VNAF mechanics earmarked to perform UH-1 repair were trained by the U.S. Army helicopter company furnishing the aircraft. But the Army maintenance concepts and organization for the various levels of maintenance were not compatible with USAF and VNAF concepts. The Army performed very little maintenance at field units, in contrast to the two air forces which had organic and field maintenance capabilities at squadron and wing levels. As a result, the VNAF squadrons required special tools and peculiar equipment in greater quantities than were available through the Army. Coincidentally, it looked as if there would be a shortage of U.S. personnel skilled in UH-1H maintenance to advise and assist. In early 1970, before activation of the eight new Phase II UH-1 Squadrons, it was "too early to completely assess the seriousness of the rotary wing maintenance problem," according to the 7AF DCS/Materiel, "but it must receive top level attention and assistance if it is not to become a major limiting factor to Phase II expansion, and beyond." This problem would demand imaginative and vigorous management. [21/]

Supply support at the Air Logistics Command demanded attention, too. The Advisory Group's Material Specialist, Col. Ralph H. Schneck, said in January 1970 that "the lack of a responsive supply system is causing problems in managing current assets and programming future requirements." Although dealing with 112,000 line items, the data base at the depot was being kept manually. The time it took to post transactions and to update the inventory was considered excessive by the Advisory Group. "Due-in" information was questionable and a follow-up method was virtually non-existent. A manual system operating on that scale could not provide management reports or point out problems. With its increased requirements, the I&M Program would be sure to compound the difficulties and perhaps put an unacceptable strain on the supply system.[22]

USAF materiel chiefs in Vietnam believed that problems could best be solved by providing the VNAF with an automatic data processing capability; consequently, a UNIVAC 1050-II was requested in October 1969 and approved by the U.S. Air Staff in December. In January 1970, a "preconversion team" arrived at Bien Hoa from the U.S. to prepare the Air Logistics Command for delivery of the computer in March.[23]

USAF advisors considered VNAF logistics a weak area which could become critical, if not watched closely as the VNAF doubled in size during the few short years of Phase II.

CHAPTER XIII

PSYCHOLOGICAL WARFARE OPERATIONS

The VNAF was given a minor role to play in carrying out psywar operations. The policies and materials for these operations came from the JGS General Political Warfare Department, which had no VNAF or Navy representation but which kept in close contact with MACV. The responsibility for fragging a leaflet drop or loudspeaker run rested with the local ARVN commander of the area in question. The role of the VNAF was limited to providing a pilot and aircraft, in almost all cases a U-17. For the VNAF, psywar was a purely operational matter. 1/

At the end of 1969, the total USAF/VNAF psywar requirement was approximately 800 loudspeaker hours and 350,000,000 leaflets a month. The VNAF was flying 17 percent of the speaker hours and dropping 6 percent of the leaflets, using 16 U-17s and, less often, Y-6 aircraft from their one reconnaissance and four liaison squadrons, one per Corps Tactical Zone. By mid-1970 the VNAF planned to modify eight additional U-17s to equip them with speakers, bringing the aircraft available for these missions to 24 U-17s. The five U-6s would be used primarily for administrative and base-support flying, only secondarily for psywar operations. 2/

The requirement for leaflet drops and speaker hours was not expected to diminish as U.S. and Allied forces withdrew from RVN. It was assumed by 7AF and AFGP planners that as long as the NVA and VC continued to fight for control of the populace, the GVN would need to continue psywar operations to attain the following goals: counter enemy propaganda exploiting U.S. troop withdrawal; erode enemy morale; enlist popular support of the GVN; and bolster RVNAF loyalty to GVN. The need for psywar was not, therefore, directly related to the level of U.S. military activity.[3/]

Based on a daily sortie rate of 1.0 for the 29 aircraft that the VNAF would have for the psywar mission, the VNAF could fly only 37 percent of the required speaker hours and deliver 9 percent of the required leaflets after Phase II of the I&M Program. By comparison, the sortie rate for VNAF U-17s averaged 0.8 percent until December 1969. If the rate were increased to 1.5 percent, the speaker hours still would be increased to only 53 percent of the requirement, and the percentage of leaflets to 12 percent.[4/] Psywar was a weak area in the planned Vietnamization program from an operational viewpoint.

The Advisory Group considered transferring 12 U-17s (being replaced by T-41 trainers) from the VNAF Air Training Center and installing loudspeaker kits in them.[5/] The U-17 and U-6 aircraft cargo capacity was too small to support more than a fraction of the psywar program; larger aircraft would do the job more efficiently. The USAF was using C-47s, C-130s, and O-2s. By the end of 1972, the VNAF would have 48 C-123s added to their existing airlift force of 16 C-47s and 16 C-119s. But using these aircraft to drop leaflets would be at the expense of airlift, a function that could become critical for the future VNAF operating alone.

The 7AF Deputy Chief of Staff for Operations recommended in December 1969 that the VNAF supplement future leaflet drop programs by using its C-47s, C-119s, and C-123s for both transport and psywar, by means of pallet kits. To correct the speaker problem, he further recommended that USAF O-2B aircraft be turned over to the VNAF as USAF Special Operations Squadrons deactivated, even though they were not programmed for turnover under the I&M Program.[6/] But the AFGP and the VNAF were resisting this receiving of aircraft in greater numbers and at different times than planned, claiming that their capability to produce aircrews and maintenance personnel was taxed to the limit. The Advisory Group also argued that a more urgent problem was educating the ARVN commanders to use the current VNAF psywar capability properly. In the IV Corps Zone, for example, the VNAF had sole responsibility for psywar flights by January 1970 and yet was undercommitted in this task.[7/]

Other VNAF activities normally associated with psychological warfare were Civic Action, the military band, cultural teams, propaganda, and "enemy-and-civil operations."[8/] All RVNAF services were directed in December 1969 to begin Civic Action programs. The VNAF already had established its "Civic Action Center" at Da Nang, which among other minor projects, had built a small number of roads to market places and given medical and dental care in villages on those occasions when surplus drugs and equipment were available. But for all practical purposes, that the VNAF had no significant Civic Action Program was understandable, considering that civilians and peasants living near VNAF bases were in many cases better off materially than most VNAF airmen. It was not easy to enlist the aid of VNAF personnel who could be seen living with their families in shacks on the bases. The budget of the VNAF had never been adequate, according to Advisory Group personnel, and since the Air Force had doubled its size, it hardly had enough funds to take care of its own. As an example, an Advisory Group officer pointed to the fact that in his own joint VNAF/USAF Psychological Warfare Office at VNAF Headquarters, three airmen slept on the floor at night. In 1969 at Tan Son Nhut, one USAF Civic Action project even had to help house new I&M recruits by setting up a "tent city." [9/]

Family allowances, such as compensation when a husband was killed, a home rocketed, or for a new baby could not be paid from appropriated funds alone, but had to be supplemented by non-appropriated welfare funds which came largely from concessions and refreshment stands on the bases, a recognized source of revenue for the services. [10/] In early 1970, psychological warfare was a weak area for the VNAF.

CHAPTER XIV

MANGEMENT OF THE PROGRAM

Because of its magnitude and complexity, the I&M Program created a pressing need to monitor the progress of projects and detect minor problems before they had an adverse effect on related projects. Such a management system was all the more vital for the VNAF--an Air Force relatively inexperienced in the use of organizing and planning systems. What the Advisory Group devised to meet this need was the Program Management System (PMS), adapted from a "Milestone" type system used for the first ATLAS missile wing. The system was basically a time-phased checklist of the actions necessary to achieve specific capabilities or facilities. The program was comprised of projects arranged in a pyramid and with a chronological pattern of action starting at the lowest levels.[1]

The system was designed to:[2]

- Force detailed planning at unit level to carry out the broader planning formulated at headquarters.

- Insure that the project officer made up a team of the personnel contributing to the project, who would periodically review and coordinate its roles at each step in the process.

- Provide a well-defined course of action that would give continuity to projects and compensate for turnover among advisory personnel by clearly showing newcomers what had been done and what needed to be done.

- Detect problems and evaluate their effect on the ability to achieve the required capability.

At all stages in the development of a PMS project and at all working levels, Advisory Group and VNAF personnel worked together, with the

Joint I&M Management Committee at the top. All documents and project charts were designed to be read bilingually. Each project was first defined to insure that the higher levels of AFGP, the VNAF command, and the working levels had a common understanding on the precise goal for each project. The working-level people meeting together made up the list of time-phased actions designed to attain the goal. The American and Vietnamese met and discussed their needs from their various agencies, but requests and needs did not substitute for normal command actions. When problems arose, the monitors could project them at AFGP, 7AF, and VNAF staff meetings. 3/ As the Advisory Group Comptroller said: 4/

> *"The system is designed so that only the tip of the iceberg--the problem--pops out of the water. The routine actions under this system are handled at working level and the key managers are not bothered unless a problem develops. And another thing, people often forget that a strong area today can become tomorrow's weak area. PMS insures continuous monitoring of progress to insure that any weak areas are spotted promptly."*

In May 1970, a number of programs were well under way. A program for the 3d and 4th VNAF Air Divisions, with 100 projects and 850 milestones for each division, had been implemented and was actively monitored by the AFAT, VNAF, and AFGP staffs. The program for the 1st and 2d Air Divisions, of about the same size, located at the VNAF DCS/Plans Office, was to have the Vietnamese language inserted. A program for the Air Logistics Command was being reviewed in draft by the AFGP staff. And a program for the 5th Air Division was in final review by the AFGP staff. Because of the inherent flexibility of these and other PMS programs, adjustments were expected as slippages and accelerations occurred.[5/]

The advantage of the PMS was that it was simple, and the VNAF, just starting with management techniques, needed simplicity. The system forced personnel at all levels to become involved in planning--especially the people down in the unit most familiar with the job. The PMS was oriented toward the end product, the goal, and not toward a function, and it provided a day-to-day reminder of actions to be completed in a given month. Both the VNAF and Advisory Team Project Officers usually kept milestone charts on the wall by their desks. General Minh, the VNAF Commander, was enthusiastic about the Group's Program Management System, as were the VNAF officers who became involved with it. The Group's Comptroller said, "We are extremely pleased with the way the VNAF has grabbed it."[6/]

CHAPTER XV

PHASE III

In early 1970, at the close of this reporting period, it was apparent that a sizable third increment would have to be added to the RVN Armed Forces after the Phase II I&M expansion was completed. This "Phase III" was the result of revised estimates of the threat. U.S. officials in mid-1969 believed it likely that the NVA would remain in South Vietnam as U.S. force redeployments continued. The earlier hope of seeing the NVA redeploy simultaneously and the war scale down to pre-1965 insurgency was becoming less realistic. As a result of these revised estimates, Defense Secretary Laird redefined the goal of the I&M Program for the Service Secretaries and the JCS as being one of "developing an RVNAF with the capability to cope successfully with the combined Viet Cong/North Vietnamese Army threat."[1]

Throughout the end of 1969 and the first months of 1970, U.S. military planners in Vietnam and Washington, D.C. were developing proposed RVNAF force structures that would meet this goal, with no final determination made by the end of March 1970. It was already clear, however, that certain principles would be embodied in the final program:[2]

- Phase III VNAF increases would come only after completion of Phase II and would not disrupt it.

- They would bring the VNAF much closer to realistic self-sufficiency.

115

- Increases would be not only quantitative but also qualitative.

- The final posture of the VNAF would not come close to matching the combined Free World assets existing in early 1970.

- Risks would necessarily adhere in the situation following the U.S. phase-down.

As in the case of Phase II, the limiting and pacing factor was training, and the critical phase of training lay in the English language training. 3/ Training requirements for the VNAF in general were always more complex than for the other services because of the need for highly skilled technicians. 4/

The force resulting from Phase III, if proposals were accepted, would probably consist of 49 or 50 squadrons with about 1,300 aircraft, including helicopters, and 44,000 personnel--an increase of 9 or 10 squadrons, 350 aircraft, and 7,500 personnel over the final Phase II force. Improvement of the VNAF had to be qualitative as well. Because of the limitations imposed by manpower and training, qualitative approaches included:

- Enlarging of squadrons to have the same command and administrative personnel responsible for more equipment and personnel.

- Keeping the number of bases the same (seven).

- Increasing the force selectively to expand those tactical functions which would do the most toward finding and destroying the enemy's main force units in the field.

It would be possible to expand the squadrons because, unlike the USAF, VNAF operations called for little unit mobility or TDY; the aircraft always flew from the same base. Phase III could be looked upon as an attempt to increase effectiveness of the VNAF, as much as one to increase its size. It could be carried out in approximately 18 months.[5]

If 7AF's recommendations were approved, the 20-25 percent increase in VNAF aircraft and personnel would mean specifically one more FAC and VR (liaison) squadrons, two fighter squadrons, two C-7 airlift squadrons, five helicopter squadrons, an expansion of two of the existing airlift squadrons and eight of the fighter squadrons, and convertible gunship packages for two airlift squadrons.[6] As the 7AF Director of Plans said, "The increase has to be consistent with what the VNAF can absorb. In that light, what we propose is realistic."[7] At the end of Phase III, the VNAF would have 52 percent of the 1969 combined USAF and VNAF fixed-wing capability, and 20 percent of the USAF and U.S. Army rotary wing. It would be able to maintain the 1969 level of activity only by increasing its sortie rates by 93 percent. Thus in FY 1973 and afterward, if enemy activity remained at 1969 levels, the same degree of security could not be maintained.

According to Phase III studies, however, security would be determined not only by the level of enemy activity, but also by "RVNAF improvement in capability, rate of progress in the pacification program, and level of U.S. forces remaining." One proposal was a transitional USAF force to

9. (C) Wuerz Interview.

10.   Ibid.

11.   Ibid.

12. (C) Ibid;
    (C) LaRocco Interview.

13. (C) Wuerz Interview.

14. (S) Training Plan, VNAF/7AF/AFGP, subj: VNAF TACS ALO/FAC Upgrading Plan, Mar 69.

15.   Ibid.

16. (C) Wuerz Interview.

17.   Ibid.

18. (S) Ltr, 7AF (TACD) to DOA, subj: Request for Input to CHECO Report, undated;
    (TS) RVNAF Vietnamization Study, 23 Dec 69.

19. (S) Training Plan, VNAF/7AF/AFGP, subj: VNAF TACS ALO/FAC Upgrading Plan, Mar 69.
    (C) Wuerz Interview.

20. (C) Wuerz Interview.

21. (S) Training Plan, VNAF/7AF/AFGP, subj: VNAF TACS ALO/FAC Upgrading Plan, Mar 69.

22. (S) Management Book, I&M Program, AFGP, 10 Jan 70.

23. (S) Interview, Maj Jack H. Taylor, AFGP-ODC, with J. T. Bear, 8 Apr 70. (Hereafter cited: Taylor Interview.)

24. (S) Fact Book.

25. (S) Taylor Interview.

26.   Ibid.

27.   Ibid.

28. (S) Briefing, Ops-Plans, AFGP (ODC), for Vice Comdr., PACAF, Jan 70. (Hereafter cited: Vice Comdr, PACAF, Briefing.)

29. (S)   Ltr, 7AF (TACD) to DOA, subj: Request for Input to CHECO Report, undated.

30.   Ibid.

31. (S)   Interview, Lt Col Malcolm S. Bounds, Chief, Weapons and Force Plans Branch, TACC, with J. T. Bear, 14 Apr 70. (Hereafter cited: Bounds Interview.)

32. (S)   Ltr, 7AF (TACD) to DOA, subj: Request for Input to CHECO Report, undated;
    (S)   Taylor Interview.

33. (S)   Ltr, 7AF (TACD) to DOA, subj: Request for Input to CHECO Report, undated;
    (S)   Bounds Interview.

34. (S)   Ltr, 7AF (TACD) to DOA, subj: Request for Input to CHECO Report, undated;
    (S)   Vice Comdr, PACAF, Briefing.

35.   Ibid.

36. (S)   Bounds Interview.

37. (S)   Ltr, 7AF (TACD) to DOA, subj: Request for Input to CHECO Report, undated.

38. (S)   Ibid;
    (S)   Taylor Interview.

39. (S)   CHECO Rprt, Hq PACAF, DOTEC, "IV DASC, Operations, 1965-1969," 1 Aug 69. (Hereafter cited: "IV DASC.")

40.   Ibid.

41. (C)   End-of-Tour Rprt, Chief, AFAT-7, Col Delbert J. Light, Aug 69.

42. (S)   "IV DASC."

43. (S)   Ltr, 7AF (TACD) to DOA, subj: Request for Input to CHECO Report, undated.

44. (S)   "Trends, Indicators, and Analyses", May 69.

45. (S)   "IV DASC."

46. (C)   End-of-Tour Rprt, Chief, AFAT-7, Col Delbert J. Light, Aug 69.

47.   Ibid.

48. (S)   "IV DASC."

49. (C)   Memo, AFGP-ODC to 7AF-DPLR, subj: Required Operation Capability--VNAF Night FAC Capability, 26 Dec 69.

50. (C)   Ltr, Col William R. Grier Jr., AFGP (ODC) to DCS/Ops, Hq VNAF, subj: Night FAC and Fighter Capability, 9 Jan 70.

51.   Ibid.

52. (C)   Wuerz Interview.

53. (C)   Memo, Director of Ops, AFGP, to Chief, AFGP, subj: Required Operational Capability--VNAF FAC Capability, 29 Dec 69.

54. (C)   Memo, Lt Col A. H. Wuerz Jr., Ops Staff Advisor (TACS) to Col W. R. Grier, Director of Ops Planning, AFGP, subj: ALO/FAC Program--End of year report, 1969.

55.   Ibid.

CHAPTER VI

1. (C)   Interview, Lt Col C. E. Davis, AFGP-ODC, with J. T. Bear, 28 Feb 70.

2. (S)   Brig General Young Interview, 29 Dec 69.

3.   Ibid.

4. (S)   Rprt, Hq USAF, USAF Management Summary, SEA, 9 Dec 69.

5. (S)   Carson End-of-Tour Rprt.

6. (S)   End-of-Tour Rprt, Brig Gen A. W. Schinz, Chief, AFGP, 1966.

7. (TS) History Rprt, MACV, 1966.

8.   Ibid.

9. (C)   Rprt, Hq USAF, Combat Evaluation of the F-5 Aircraft, Apr 66.

10.   Ibid;
    (S) DPLFS Letter.

11. (C)   Rprt, Hq USAF, Combat Evaluation of the F-5 Aircraft, Apr 66.
12.   Ibid.
13. (S)   Monthly History Rprts, AFGP, 1965-1968.
14. (C)   Interview, Lt Col C. E. Davis, AFGP-ODC, with J. T. Bear, 28 Feb 70.
15. (S)   Rprt, AFGP Modernization Programming Status, 16 Feb 67.
16. (S)   Monthly Histories, AFGP, 1965-1968.
17. (S)   VNAF Status Review, Jan 70, AFGP-DCR.
18. (S)   Monthly History Rprts, AFGP, 1965-1968.
19.   Ibid.
20.   Ibid.
21. (U)   Rprt, Tactical Fighter Weapons Center (TAC), COMBAT DRAGON, Apr 68.
22.   Ibid.
23. (S)   Monthly History Rprts, AFGP, 1967.
24. (U)   Article, "Air Force and Space Digest," Sep 69.
25. (C)   Ltr, AFGP-ODC to 7AF-DOA, subj: Input for CHECO Report, 8 Jan 70.
26. (S)   Carson End-of-Tour Rprt, 5 Aug 69.
27. (U)   News Release, No. 9-168-11, Hq 7AF, Director of Information.
28.   Ibid.
29. (C)   Interview, Lt Col C. E. Davis, AFGP-ODC, with J. T. Bear, 28 Feb 70.
30. (U)   Article, "Air Force and Space Digest Almanac," Sep 69.
31. (S)   Rprt, MAP, Military Assistance Program Report, RCS: AF-V12, 24 Jan 70.
32. (S/NF) "Organization, Mission, and Growth of VNAF, 1949-1968."

33. (S)   Rprt, Hq USAF, USAF Management Summary, SEA, 9 Dec 69.

34. (S)   Study, 7AF, VNAF I&M, Phase III and Related Planning, 15 Jan 70, Annex D.

35. (S/NF) "Organization, Mission, and Growth, of VNAF, 1949-1968."

36.   Ibid.

37.   Ibid.

38. (S)   Brig General Young Interview, 29 Dec 69.

39. (S)   Interview, Gen C. W. Abrams, Jr., COMUSMACV, with Kenneth Sams, 3 Mar 70.

40. (S)   VNAF Status Review, AFGP-DCR, Jan 70.

41. (S)   Rprt, AFGP-DCR, VNAF Statistical Summary, Jan 69.

42. (C)   Interview, Lt Col V. E. Davis, AFGP-ODC, with J. T. Bear, 28 Feb 70.

43.   Ibid.

44. (C)   End-of-Tour Rprt, Director of Ops, AFGP, Col J. C. Neill, 3 Nov 69;
    (U)   Rprt, AFGP, I&M Program Management Summary Book, 19 Jan 70.

45. (C)   Interview, Maj John J. Lynch, AFAT-7, with C. W. Thorndale, 30 Jan 70.

46. (S/NF) "Organization, Mission, and Growth of VNAF, 1949-1968."

47. (S)   Study, VNAF I&M, Phase III and Related Planning, 15 Jan 70, Annex P.

48.   Ibid.

CHAPTER VII

1. (S)   Brig General Young, Interview, 29 Dec 68.

2. (S)   Carson End-of-Tour Rprt.

3. (S)   End-of-Tour Rprt, Col Delbert J. Light, Chief, AFAT-7, Aug 69.

4. (S)   Carson End-of-Tour Rprt.

5. (S)   VNAF Programming Plan No. 9762.

6. (S)   Rprt, 7AF Combined Campaign Plan, 1969 Qtr Report, FY 1/1970, Tab B.

7. (S)   Ltr, Gen C. W. Abrams, Jr., COMUSMACV, to Gen Cao Van Vien, Chief, JGS, 29 Jan 69.

8. (S)   Study, Hq 7AF, VNAF I&M, Phase III and Related Planning, 15 Jan 70, Annex H.

9.   Ibid.

10.   Ibid.

11. (S)   End-of-Tour Rprt, Col Delbert J. Light, Chief, AFAT-7, Aug 69.

12. (S)   Carson End-of-Tour Rprt.

13. (S)   Rprt, 7AF Combined Campaign Plan 1969 Quarterly Report (FY-2/69).

14. (S)   Carson End-of-Tour Rprt.

15. (S)   Interview, Lt Col J. V. Woodmansee, USA, 164th Combat Aviation, with C. W. Thorndale, 2 Feb 70;
    (S)   Interviews, Maj W. Smith, USA, and Capt C. T. Akin, USA, Advisors, 21st ARVN Div, with C. W. Thorndale, 4 Feb 70.

16. (S)   Interview, Maj R. N. Cherry and S. A. Mazur, AFGP, and Maj P. L. Parker, USA, Hq VNAF, with J. T. Bear, 2 Mar 70.

17.   Ibid.

18. (C)   Interview, Lt Col R. W. Dupras, USAF, Dep Dir, IV DASC, Can Tho, with C. W. Thorndale, 2 Feb 70;
    (S)   Interview, Maj P. L. Parker, USA, with J. T. Bear, 2 Mar 70.

19. (S)   End-of-Tour Rprt, Col John C. Neill, Director of Operations, AFGP, 3 Nov 69.

20.   Ibid.

21.   Ibid.

22. (S)   End-of-Tour Rprt, Col Delbert J. Light, Chief, AFAT-7, Aug 69.

23. (S)   End-of-Tour Rprt, Col John C. Neill, Director of Operations, AFGP, 3 Nov 69.

24.   Ibid.

25. (C)   VNAF/AFGP/USARV I&M Helicopter Augmentation Plan, No. 70-51, Proposed to MACV, Feb 70.

26.   Ibid.

27.   Ibid.

28.   Ibid.

29.   Ibid.

30.   Ibid.

31. (S)   End-of-Tour Rprt, Col John C. Neill, Director of Operations, AFGP, 3 Nov 69.

32.   Ibid.

33. (S)   Rprt, MAP, RCS: AF-V 12; AFGP, 24 Jan 70.

34. (S)   End-of-Tour Rprt, Col John C. Neill, Director of Operations, AFGP, 3 Nov 69.

35.   Ibid.

36. (S)   Rprt, MAP, RCS: AF-V 12, AFGP, 24 Jan 70.

CHAPTER VIII

1. (TS)   Study, VNAF I&M, Hq 7AF, 23 Dec 69.

2. (C)   End-of-Tour Rprt, Chief, AFAT-1, Col H. H. D. Heilberg, Jr., 30 Oct 69;
   (S)   Rprt, AFGP-ODC, Historical Summary, Jan 70, 19 Feb 70.

3. (S)   Interview, Col Senour Hunt, Chief, AFAT-1, and Lt Col Roger Pagels, AFAT-1, with J. T. Bear, 9 Feb 70. (Hereafter cited: Hunt and Pagels Interview.)

4.   Ibid.

5. (S)   Rprt, AFGP, 7AF Combined Campaign Plan 1969, Quarterly Rprt (FY 4/1969), Tab B.

6. (S)   Hunt and Pagels Interview.

7.   Ibid.

8. (U)   Correspondence, Recommendation for Decoration for Maj Nguyen Que Son, AFAT-1, undated.

9.   Ibid.

10.   Ibid.

11. (C) End-of-Tour Rprt, Chief, AFAT-1, Col H. H. D. Heilberg, Jr., 30 Oct 69.

12. (S) Brig General Young Interview, 29 Dec 69.

13. (S) Study, Hq 7AF, VNAF I&M Phase III and Related Planning, 15 Jan 70, Annex H.

14. (C) End-of-Tour Rprt, AFGP-ODC, Col J. C. Neill, 3 Nov 69.

CHAPTER IX

1. (U)   Rprt, "South Vietnam's Robust Teenage Air Force," AFGP, May 66.

2. (S)   End-of-Tour Rprt, Brig Gen A. W. Schinz, Oct 66.

3. (C)   End-of-Tour Rprt, Col H. H. D. Heilberg, Jr., Chief, AFAT-1, 30 Oct 69;
   (S)   VNAF Status Review, AFGP, Jan 70.

4. (S)   Rprt, MAP, RCS: AF-V12, 24 Jan 70.

5. (C)   End-of-Tour Rprt, Col H. H. D. Heilberg, Jr., Chief, AFAT-1, 30 Oct 69.

6.   Ibid.

7. (S)   Study, Hq 7AF, Phase III and Related Planning, 15 Jan 70, Annex P.

8. (S)   VNAF Statistical Summary, AFGP-DCR, Nov 69.

9. (S)   Study, Hq 7AF, Phase III and Related Planning, 15 Jan 70, Annex P.

10. (S)   Hunt and Pagels Interview.

11. (S)   Study, Hq 7AF, Phase III and Related Planning, 15 Jan 70, Annex P.

12. (S)   Rprt, AFGP, 7AF Combined Campaign Plan 1969, Qtr Rprt, FY 2/1970;
    (C)   End-of-Tour Rprt, Col H. H. D. Heilbert, Jr., Chief, AFAT-1, 30 Oct 69.

13.   Ibid.

14.   Ibid.

15. (C)   Memo, DOA to DCS/Ops, subj: Study of Air America Operations, 16 Jan 70.

16. (S)   Talking Paper, AFGP-XPR for Comdr, 7AF, 27 Nov 69.

17. (S/NF) Msg, 7AF to CSAF, subj: VNAF Airlift Force Structure, 18/1127 Feb 70.

18.   Ibid.

19. (S)   Msg, CINCPACAF to 7AF, subj: VNAF Airlift Force Structure 070300Z Mar 70.

20. (S)   Study, Hq 7AF, DPL-70-094, VNAF Airlift.

CHAPTER X

1. (S)   Interview, Lt Col Roger E. Pagels, AFAT-1, with J. T. Bear, 19 Feb 70.

2. (S)   Study, Hq 7AF, VNAF I&M, Phase III and Related Planning, 15 Jan 70, Annexes A through P; Z.

3. (S)   Briefing Book, AFAT-1, Mission of 716th Recon Sq.

4. (S)   Interview, Lt Col Roger E. Pagels, AFAT-1, with J. T. Bear, 19 Feb 70.

5.   Ibid.

6. (U)   Ltr, CS/7AF to AFGP, subj: Facility Requirements for VNAF I&M Program;
   (S)   Ltr, DI to DOTE, Hq PACAF, subj: Project CHECO Rprt - VNAF I&M Program (U), 7 Jul 70.

136

7. (S) Study, Hq 7AF, VNAF I&M, Phase III and Related Planning, 15 Jan 70, Annexes A through P; Z.

8. Ibid.

9. Ibid;
   (S) Ltr, MACV-MA to CINCPACAF, subj: RVN Force Structure Increase Proposals and Requests of Improvement of Living Standards, 25 Mar 70.

10. Ibid.

11. Ibid.

12. Ibid.

13. Ibid.

14. (TS) Study, Hq 7AF, VNAF I&M, Phase III and Related Planning, 23 Dec 69.

CHAPTER XI

1. (S) Talking Papers and Research Data, 7AF, DPLP for Comdr, 7AF, 17, 19 Jan 70.

2. (S) Brig General Young Interview, 29 Dec 69.

3. (S) Rprt, Hq 7AF, Combined Campaign Plan 1969, Qtr Rprt, FY 2/1970, Tab B;
   (S) Rprt, AFGP Historical Summary, Jan 70.

4. (S) Ltr, 7AF, DPL, to DOA, Input to CHECO Rprt, 7 Jan 70.

5. (S) Plan, 7AF, FY 1976 Force Improvement Plan, Annex K. The VNAF.

6. (S) Ltr, 7AF, DPL, to DOA, Input to CHECO Rprt, 7 Jan 70.

7. (S) Talking Papers and Research Data, 7AF, DPLP, for 7AF Comdr, 19 Jan 70.

8. Ibid.

9. Ibid.

10. (S) Carson End-of-Tour Report.

11. (S)   Plan, 7AF, FY 1976 Force Improvement Plan, Annex K, The VNAF.

12. (S)   Talking Papers and Research Data, 7AF, DPLP, for 7AF Comdr, 19 Jan 70.

CHAPTER XII

1. (U)   News Item, "U.S. Stars and Stripes," statement by AF Secretary Robert C. Seamans, Jr., 30 Jan 70.

2. (S)   Study, Hq 7AF, VNAF I&M, Phase III and Related Planning, 15 Jan 70, Annexes A through P; Z.

3. (C)   Plan, KE-HOACH 69-17, VNAF, 1 Aug 69.

4. (S)   Brig General Young Interview, 29 Jan 70.

5. (S)   Study, Hq 7AF, VNAF I&M, Phase III and Related Planning, 15 Jan 70, Annexes A through P; Z.

6.   Ibid.

7. (S/NF)   "Organization, Mission, and Growth of VNAF, 1949-1968."

8. (C)   Interview, Maj John J. Lynch, AFAT-7, with C. W. Thorndale, 30 Jan 70;
   (C)   Interview, MSgt R. Hauer, AFAT-7, with C. W. Thorndale, 31 Jan 70.

9. (S)   End-of-Tour Rprt, Brig Gen Donovan F. Smith, Chief, AFGP, Mar 68.

10. (U)   I&M Program Management Book, AFGP, 10 Jan 70.

11. (S)   Study 7AF, VNAF I&M, Phase III and Related Planning, 15 Jan 70, Annexes A through P; Z.

12. (S)   Rprts, 7AF, Combined Campaign Plan 1969, Qtr Rprts;
    (C)   End-of-Tour Rprt, Col George E. Hoffman, Jr., Director of Materiel, AFGP, Sep 69;
    (S)   Carson End-of-Tour Rprt.

13.   Ibid.

14.   Ibid.

15. (S) Rprts, 7AF, Combined Campaign Plan 1969, Qtr Reports.
16. (S) Study, 7AF, VNAF I&M, Phase III and Related Planning, 15 Jan 70, Annexes A through P; Z.
17. Ibid.
18. (S) Rprt, MAP, RCS: AF-V12, AFGP, 24 Jan 70.
19. (C) End-of-Tour Rprt, Col George E. Hoffman, Jr., Director of Materiel, AFGP, Sep 69.
20. (S) End of Tour Rprt, Col H. H. D. Heilberg, Jr., Chief, AFAT-1, 30 Oct 69.
21. (S) Study, 7AF VNAF I&M, Phase III and Related Planning, 15 Jan 70, Annexes A through P; Z.
22. (S) Talking Papers, Director, AFGP-MDC, for 7AF Comdr, 12 Jan 70.
23. Ibid.

CHAPTER XIII

1. (C) Interview, Lt Col Kenneth Brown, AFGP Advisor for PsyOps, VNAF Hq, with J. T. Bear, 7 Feb 70.
2. (S) Study, Hq 7AF, VNAF I&M, Phase III and Related Planning, 15 Jan 70, Annex H.
3. Ibid.
4. Ibid.
5. (C) Interview, Lt Col Kenneth Brown, AFGP Advisor for PsyOps, VNAF Hq with J. T. Bear, 7 Feb 70.
6. (S) Study, Hq 7AF, VNAF I&M, Phase III and Related Planning, 15 Jan 70, Annex H.
7. (C) Interview, Lt Col Kenneth Brown, AFGP Advisor for PsyOps, VNAF Hq, with J. T. Bear, 7 Feb 70.
8. Ibid.
9. Ibid.
10. Ibid.

CHAPTER XIV

1. (U) Interview, Col Mark W. Gillaspie, Comptroller, AFGP, with J. T. Bear, 16 May 70. (Hereafter cited: Gillaspie Interview.)

2. (U) Briefing, AFGP, Program Management System, Apr 70.

3. (U) Gillaspie Interview.

4. (U) Ibid.

5. (U) Briefing, AFGP, Program Management System, Apr 70.

6. (U) Gillaspie Interview.

CHAPTER XV

1. (S) Memo, Secretary of Defense to Service Secretaries and CJCS, subj: Government of Vietnam Proposals Presented at Midway Conference, 8 Jun 69, 12 Aug 69.

2. (S) Talking Papers, AFGP-XPR and 7AF (DPLP), for 7AF Comdr, 16-19 Jan 70.

3. Ibid.

4. (TS) Study, Hq 7AF, Phase III and Related Planning, 23 Dec 69.

5. Ibid.

6. Ibid.

7. (S) Interview, Col Frank G. Lester, 7AF, Director of Plans, with J. T. Bear, 27 Feb 70.

8. (TS) Study, Hq 7AF, Phase III and Related Planning, 23 Dec 69.

9. Ibid, App I to Annex P.

10. (S) CHECO Digest, Feb 68.

11. (S) Interview, Col Frank G. Lester, 7AF, Director of Plans, with J. T. Bear, 27 Feb 70.

12. (TS) Study, Hq 7AF, Phase III and Related Planning, 23 Dec 69.

13. Ibid.

APPENDIX I
VNAF HEADQUARTERS

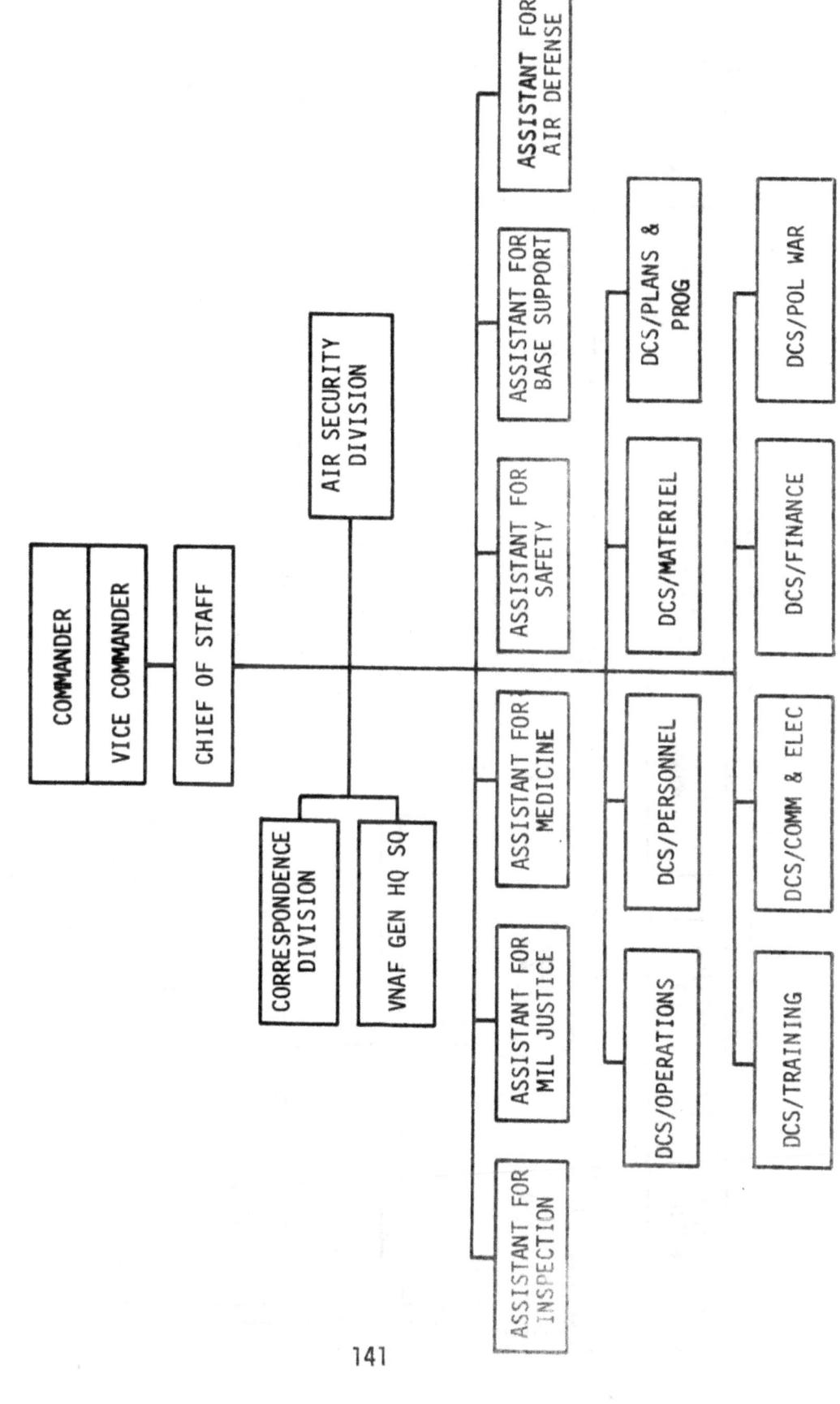

SOURCE: VNAF Status Review, Jan 70

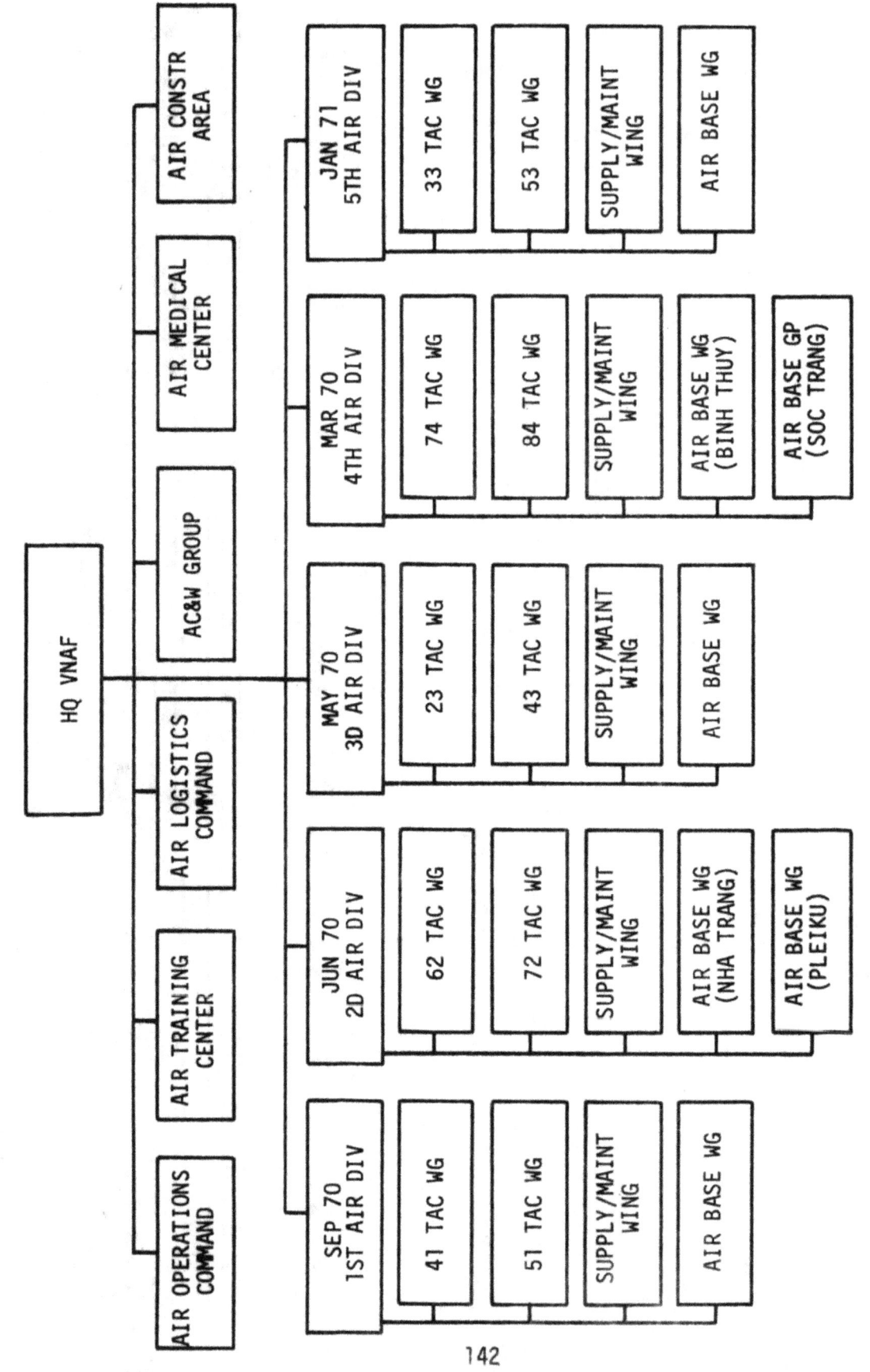

SOURCE: VNAF Status Review, Jan 70

APPENDIX III

TYPICAL VNAF AIR DIVISION ORGANIZATIONAL CHART

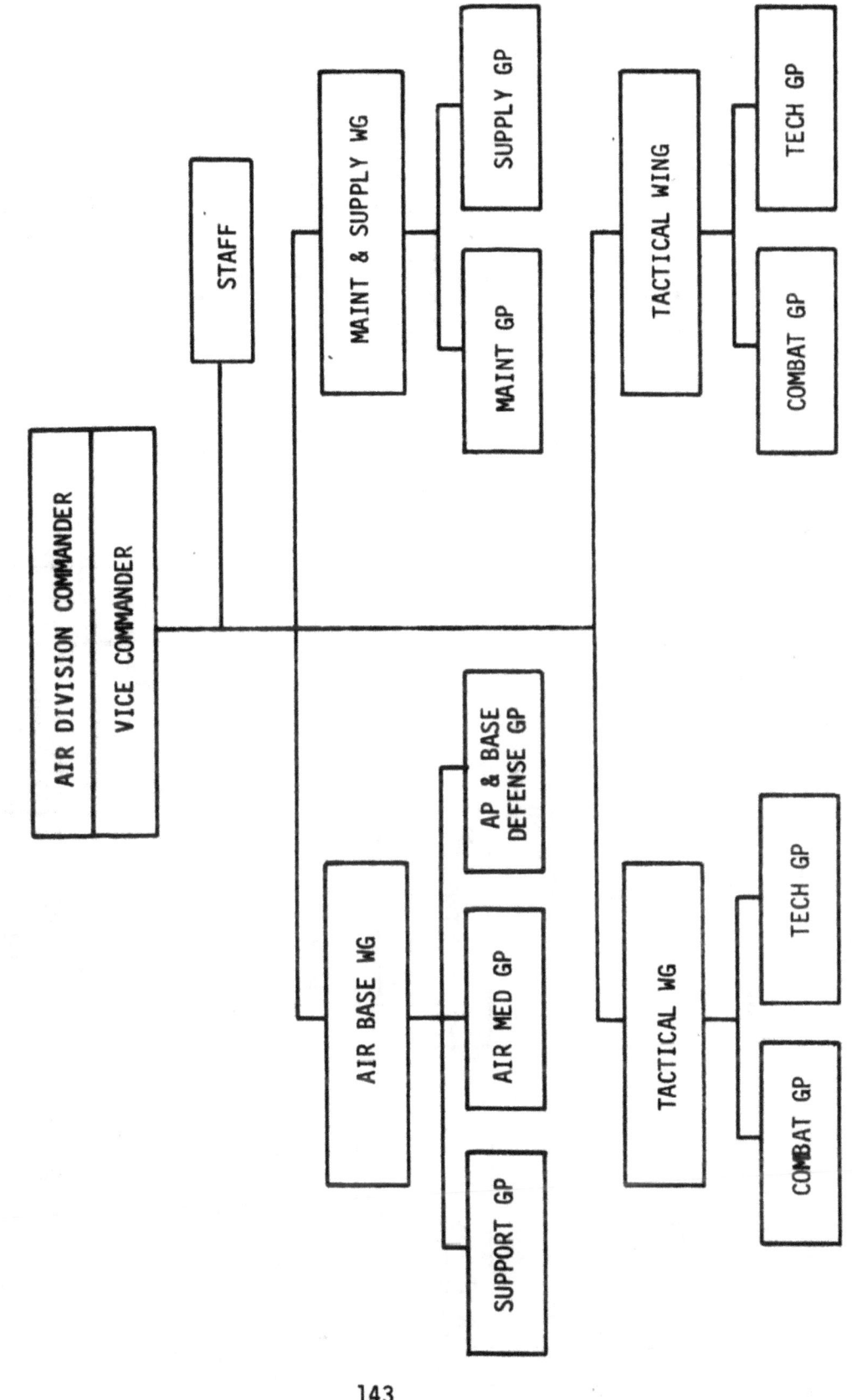

NOTE: Slight variations exist for Air Divs supporting Tactical Wgs at different locations.
SOURCE: VNAF Status Review, Jan '70

APPENDIX IV
AIR LOGISTICS COMMAND

```
                    ┌─────────────────────────┐
                    │ COMMANDER               │
                    │ DEPUTY COMMANDER        │
                    └───────────┬─────────────┘
                                │
                        ┌───────┴────────┐
                        │   POLWAR DIV   │
                        └────────────────┘
                                │
                    ┌───────────┴─────────────┐
                    │    CHIEF OF STAFF       │
                    └───────────┬─────────────┘
                                │
          ┌──────────┬──────────┼──────────┬──────────────────┐
          │          │          │          │                  │
  ┌───────┴──────┐   │   ┌──────┴──────┐   │           ┌──────┴──────────┐
  │ ASST FOR     │   │   │ ASST FOR    │   │           │ GROUND SAFETY   │
  │ INSPECTION   │   │   │ PLANS & MGMT│   │           │ OFFICE          │
  └──────────────┘   │   └─────────────┘   │           └─────────────────┘
                     │                     │
              ┌──────┴──────┐       ┌──────┴──────┐
              │ COMPTROLLER │       │  TRAINING   │
              │             │       │   OFFICE    │
              └─────────────┘       └─────────────┘
```

- PERSONNEL OFFICE
- FINANCE OFFICE
- MAINT ENG WING
  - Acft & Prop Repair Gp
  - Fabr & Acft Support Equip Gp
- SUPPLY & TRANS CENTER
  - MGMT Service Div
  - MATL Fac Sq
  - Transportation Ops & Spt Sq
- MATL MGMT CENTER
  - Log MGMT Div
  - MATL Ctl Div
  - Support SVS Div
- SUPPORT GROUP
  - Supply SVS Det
  - Supply Sq
  - Vehicle Sq
  - Civil Eng Sq
  - AP & Int Sec Det

SOURCE: VNAF Status Review, Jan 70

144

APPENDIX V
VNAF BEDDOWN LOCATIONS

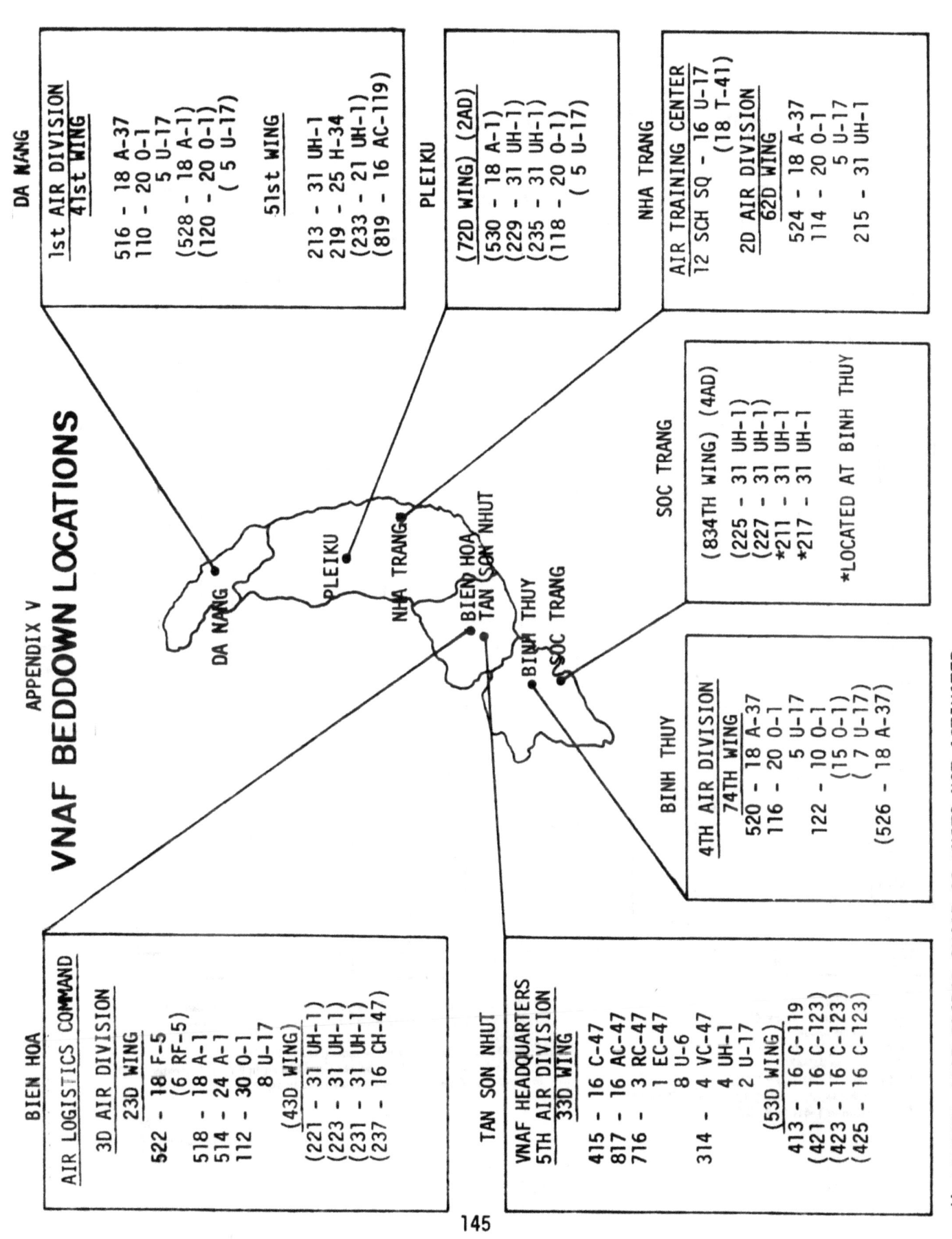

DA NANG

1st AIR DIVISION
41st WING

- 516 - 18 A-37
- 110 - 20 O-1
- 5 U-17
- (528 - 18 A-1)
- (120 - 20 O-1)
- (5 U-17)

51st WING

- 213 - 31 UH-1
- 219 - 25 H-34
- (233 - 21 UH-1)
- (819 - 16 AC-119)

PLEIKU

(72D WING) (2AD)
- (530 - 18 A-1)
- (229 - 31 UH-1)
- (235 - 31 UH-1)
- (118 - 20 O-1)
- (5 U-17)

NHA TRANG

AIR TRAINING CENTER
- 12 SCH SQ - 16 U-17
- (18 T-41)

2D AIR DIVISION
62D WING

- 524 - 18 A-37
- 114 - 20 O-1
- 5 U-17
- 215 - 31 UH-1

SOC TRANG

(834TH WING) (4AD)
- (225 - 31 UH-1)
- (227 - 31 UH-1)
- *211 - 31 UH-1
- *217 - 31 UH-1

*LOCATED AT BINH THUY

BINH THUY

4TH AIR DIVISION
74TH WING

- 520 - 18 A-37
- 116 - 20 O-1
- 5 U-17
- 122 - 10 O-1
- (15 O-1)
- (7 U-17)
- (526 - 18 A-37)

BIEN HOA

AIR LOGISTICS COMMAND
3D AIR DIVISION
23D WING

- 522 - 18 F-5
- (6 RF-5)
- 518 - 18 A-1
- 514 - 24 A-1
- 112 - 30 O-1
- 8 U-17

(43D WING)
- (221 - 31 UH-1)
- (223 - 31 UH-1)
- (231 - 31 UH-1)
- (237 - 16 CH-47)

TAN SON NHUT

VNAF HEADQUARTERS
5TH AIR DIVISION
33D WING

- 415 - 16 C-47
- 817 - 16 AC-47
- 716 - 3 RC-47
- 1 EC-47
- 8 U-6
- 314 - 4 VC-47
- 4 UH-1
- 2 U-17

(53D WING)
- 413 - 16 C-119
- (421 - 16 C-123)
- (423 - 16 C-123)
- (425 - 16 C-123)

( ) DENOTES ACCELERATED PHASE II UNITS NOT ACTIVATED

APPENDIX VI

VNAF IMPROVEMENT AND MODERNIZATION PLAN

	PRE I & M FORCES			ADDITIVE FORCES				TOTAL FORCE		FY SQ ACTIVATION				
				PHASE I		PHASE II		FY 2/72						
	SQ	UE	ACFT AUTH	SQ	ACFT AUTH	SQ	ACFT AUTH	SQ	ACFT AUTH	68[1]	69	70	71	72
TACTICAL														
F-5	1	18	18					1	18	1				
A-1/A-37 [2]	3	18	54			1	18	4	72		3			1
A-1	1	18	18			2	36	3	54	1				2
A-1	1	24	24					1	24	1				
HELICOPTER														
H-34/UH-1H [2]	4	20[3]	80		44			4	124		4			
UH-1H				4	124[6]	4	124[6]	8	248				8	
H-34	1	25	25					1	25	1				
CH-47						1	16	1	16				1	
TRANSPORT														
C-47	1	16	16					1	16	1				
C-119	1	16	16					1	16	1				
C-123						3	48	3	48					3
SAM [4]						1	10	1	10		1			
GUNSHIP														
AC-47 [2]	1	16	16					1	16		1			
AC-119						1	16	1	16					1
LIAISON														
O-1/U-17 [8]						1	30	1	30				1	
O-1/U-17 [9]						1	25	1	25			1		
O-1/U-17 [10]						1	20	1	20				1	
O-1/U-17	4	30[7]	120					4	120	4				
TRAINING														
U-17 [5]	1	16	16	-1	-16									
T-41				1	18			1	18	1				
RECON	1							1		1				
RF-5A							6		6					
EC-47		1	1						1					
RC-47		3	3						3					
U-6A		8	8						8					
TOTAL	20	-	415	4	170	16	349	40	934	12	9	1	11	7

[1] FY 68 or Prior
[2] Aircraft converted in FY 69.
   3 A-1 sqs to A-37s
   4 H-34 sqs to UH-1s
   1 C-47 Sq to AC-47
[3] UE Increases to 31 in FY 3/70.
[4] Special Air Mission, 4 VC-47, 4 UH-1, 2 U-17.
[5] Conversion to T-41s in FY 3/70.
[6] 80 Acft are transports, 32 are gunships, 12 Command & Control.
[7] 20 - O-1 and 10 - U-17 aircraft. UE changes to 20 O-1 and 5 U-17's in FY 71.
[8] 30 O-1s. Eight U-17's to be reassigned to Sq in FY 71
[9] 25 O-1s. Seven U-17's to be reassigned to Sq in FY 71. Activated 3/70
[10] 20 O-1's. Five U-17's to be reassigned to Sq in FY 71

Source: JCS-M COMUSMACV

APPENDIX VII

SOURCE OF PHASE I & II VNAF UE AIRCRAFT

UNIT	LOCATION	A/C	UE	ACTIVATION DATE	SOURCE
223 Helo Sq	Bien Hoa	UH-1	31	1/71	190th AHC, USAR
225 Helo Sq	Soc Trang	UH-1	31	2/71	121st AHC, USAR
227 Helo Sq	Soc Trang	UH-1	31	2/71	336th AHC, USAR
229 Helo Sq	Pleiku	UH-1	31	2/71	189th AHC, USAR
221 Helo Sq	Bien Hoa	UH-1	31	3/71	68th AHC, USAR
231 Helo Sq	Bien Hoa	UH-1	31	3/71	118th AHC, USAR
233 Helo Sq	Da Nang	UH-1	31	3/71	282nd AHC, USAR
235 Helo Sq	Pleiku	UH-1	31	3/71	170th AHC, USAR
237 Helo Sq	Bien Hoa	CH-47	16	3/71	205th AHSC - USAR
118 LN Sq	Pleiku	O-1	20	4/71	19th TASS - USAF
120 LN Sq	Da Nang	O-1	20	4/71	22nd TASS - USAF
122 LN Sq	Binh Thuy	O-1	25	4/71	19th TASS - USAF
526 TFS	Binh Thuy	A-37	18	1/72	8th AS, USAF
528 TFS	Da Nang	A-1	18	1/72	602nd SOS, USAF
530 TFS	Pleiku	A-1	18	1/72	1st SOS, USAF
819 Trans Sq	Da Nang	AC-119G	16	1/72	17 SOS, USAF
421 Trans Sq	Tan Son Nhut	C-123	16	2/72	310th TAS, USAF
423 Trans Sq	Tan Son Nhut	C-123	16	2/72	311th TAS, USAF
425 Trans Sq	Tan Son Nhut	C-123	16	2/72	19th TAS, USAF

Source: COMUSMACV

APPENDIX VIII

COMPOSITION OF VIETNAM AIR FORCE

UNITS	LOCATION	TYPE ACFT	UE	ACFT POSS AS OF 31 Dec	FY 70 1	FY 70 2	FY 70 3	FY 70 4	FY 71 1	FY 71 2	FY 71 3	FY 71 4	FY 72	SOURCE	ACFT READY	CREWS READY	C-RTNG
1st Air Div	Da Nang																
41st Tac Wg	Da Nang														15	33	C-2
110 LNS	Da Nang	O-1	20	17											8	0	C-2
	Da Nang	U-17	5	8													
120 LNS	Da Nang	O-1	20	-									20	USAF Inventory			
	Da Nang	U-17	5	-										VNAF Redistribution			
516 FS	Da Nang	A-37	18	17											14	23	C-1
528 FS	Da Nang	A-1	18	-									18	602 SOS, USAF			
51st Tac Wg	Da Nang																
213 Heli Sq	Da Nang	UH-1	31	18				11						Army In-Country	16	20	C-2
219 Heli Sq	Da Nang	H-34	25	24											16	26	C-2
233 Heli Sq	Da Nang	UH-1	31	-							31			282 d AHC USAR			
819 Cmbt Sq	Da Nang	AC-47	16	-									16	USAF Storage			
2 d Air Div	Nha Trang																
62nd Tac Wg	Nha Trang														16	33	C-1
114 LNS	Nha Trang	O-1	20	18											6	0	C-1
	Nha Trang	U-17	5	7													
215 Heli Sq	Nha Trang	UH-1	31	18				11						Army In-Country	13	22	C-2
524 FS	Nha Trang	A-37	18	18											15	28	C-1
72 d Tac Wg	Pleiku																
118 LNS	Pleiku	O-1	20	-									20	USAF Inventory			
	Pleiku	U-17	5											VNAF Redistribution			
229 Heli Sq	Pleiku	UH-1	31	-							31			189th AHC, USAF			
235 Heli Sq	Pleiku	UH-1	31	-								31		170th AHC, USAF			
530 FS	Pleiku	A-1	18	-									18	1st SOS, USAF			
3 d Air Div	Bien Hoa																
23 d Tac Wg	Bien Hoa														18	45	C-1
112 LNS	Bien Hoa	O-1	30	19									10	USAF Inventory	6	0	C-1
	Bien Hoa	U-17	8	7													
514 FS	Bien Hoa	A-1	24	30											26	33	C-1
518 FS	Bien Hoa	A-1	18	21											17	22	C-2
522 FS	Bien Hoa	F-5	18	16											13	28	C-1
43 d Tac Wg	Bien Hoa																
221 Heli Sq	Bien Hoa	UH-1	31	-							31			68th AHC, USAR			
223 Heli Sq	Bien Hoa	UH-1	31	-						31				190th AHC, USAR			
231 Heli Sq	Bien Hoa	UH-1	31	-							31			118th AHC, USAR			
237 Heli Sq	Bien Hoa	CH-47	16	-									16	Marine Corps In-Cntry			
4th Air Div	Binh Thuy																
74th Tac Wg	Binh Thuy																
520 FS	Binh Thuy	A-37	18	18											15	28	C-1
116 LNS	Binh Thuy	O-1	20	15											15	33	C-2
	Binh Thuy	U-17	5	8											4	0	C-2
526 FS	Binh Thuy	A-37	18	-									18	8 AS, USAF			
122 LNS	Binh Thuy	O-1	25	-									25	USAF Inventory			
	Binh Thuy	U-17	7	-										VNAF Redistribution			

SOURCE: USAF Management Summary, Jan 70

APPENDIX VIII
(Cont'd.)
COMPOSITION OF VIETNAM AIR FORCE

UNITS	LOCATION	TYPE ACFT	UE	ACFT POSS AS OF 31 Dec	FY 70 1	FY 70 2	FY 70 3	FY 70 4	FY 71 1	FY 71 2	FY 71 3	FY 71 4	FY 72	SOURCE	ACFT READY	CREWS READY	C-RTNG
4th Air Div (Cont')																	
84th Tac Wg	Soc Trang																
225 Heli Sq	Soc Trang	UH-1	31	-						31				121st AHC, USAR			
227 Heli Sq	Soc Trang	UH-1	31	-						31				336th AHC, USAR			
211 Heli Sq	Binh Thuy	UH-1	31	15			11							US Army In-Country	9	22	C-2
217 Heli Sq	Binh Thuy	UH-1	31	18			11							US Army In-Country	13	20	C-2
5th Air Div	Tan Son Nhut																
33d Tac Wg	Tan Son Nhut														21	12	C-3
415 TSP Sq	Tan Son Nhut	C-47D	16	22											15	21	C-1
417 Cmbt Sq	Tan Son Nhut	AC-47	16	15											3	4	C-1
716 Recon Sq	Tan Son Nhut	RC-47	3	3											1	1	C-1
	Tan Son Nhut	EC-47	1	1											9	8	C-1
	Tan Son Nhut	U-6	8	9					2			2	2	Production			
	Bien Hoa	RF-5	6	-											4	0	NA
314 SAM Sq	Tan Son Nhut	VC-47	4	4											4	0	NA
	Tan Son Nhut	UH-1	4	4											2	0	NA
	Tan Son Nhut	U-17	2	2													
53d Tac Wg	Tan Son Nhut														15	11	C-3
413 TSP Sq	Tan Son Nhut	C-119	16	18													
421 TSP Sq	Tan Son Nhut	C-123	16	-									16	310th SOS USAF			
423 TSP Sq	Tan Son Nhut	C-123	16	-									16	311th SOS USAF			
425 TSP Sq	Tan Son Nhut	C-123	16	-									16	19th SOS USAF			
Air Log Wg	Cam Ranh Bay (Storage)	H-34		4													NA
Air Trng Ctr	Nha Trang														15	12	NA
12 Schl Sq	Nha Trang	U-17	0	17													
	Nha Trang	T-41	18	-			4	14						Production			
TOTAL			934	411	0	4	58	2	31	93	142	77	118		344	485	

ATTRITION AIRCRAFT

TYPE ACFT	ATT	ACFT POSS AS OF 30 NOV	FY 70 1	FY 70 2	FY 70 3	FY 70 4	FY 71 1	FY 71 2	FY 71 3	FY 71 4	FY 72	FY 73	FY 74
UH-1	342	-	3	4	4	6	9	14	18	24	110	112	38
T-41	4	-			2						1	1	-
CH-53	6	-									2	2	2
A-1	13	-									-	6	7
AC-47	5	-									-	2	3
A-37	8	-									-	4	4
C-123	1	-									-	-	1
O-1	30	-									10	10	10
VC-47	1	-									-	-	1
RF-5	3	-									3	-	-
TOTAL ATTRITION	413		3	4	6	6	9	14	18	24	126	137	66
TOTAL AIRCRAFT	1347	411	3	8	64	8	40	107	160	101	244	137	66

Source: VNAF FORSTAT, 31 Dec 69

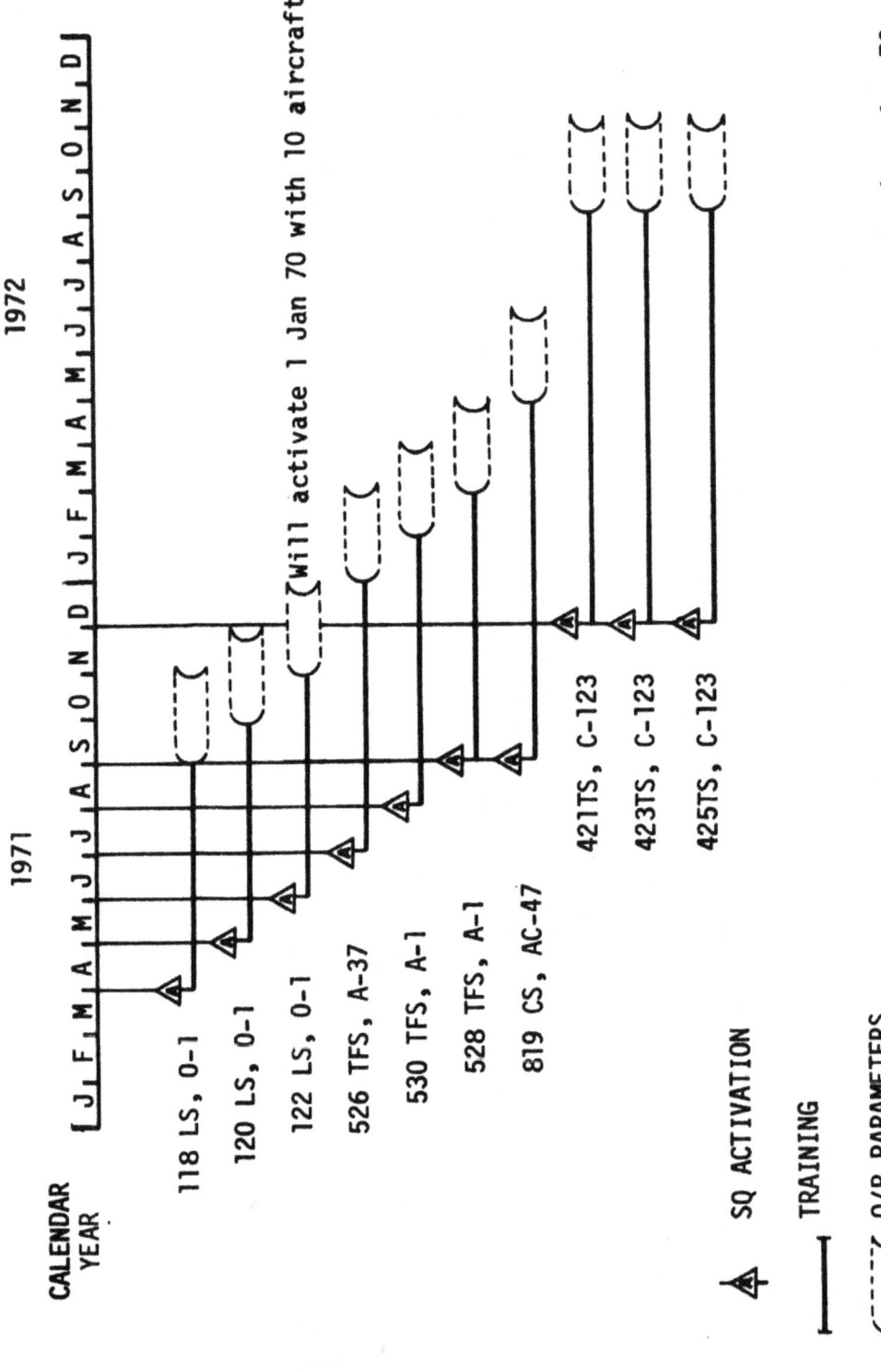

APPENDIX X

HELICOPTER ACTIVATIONS

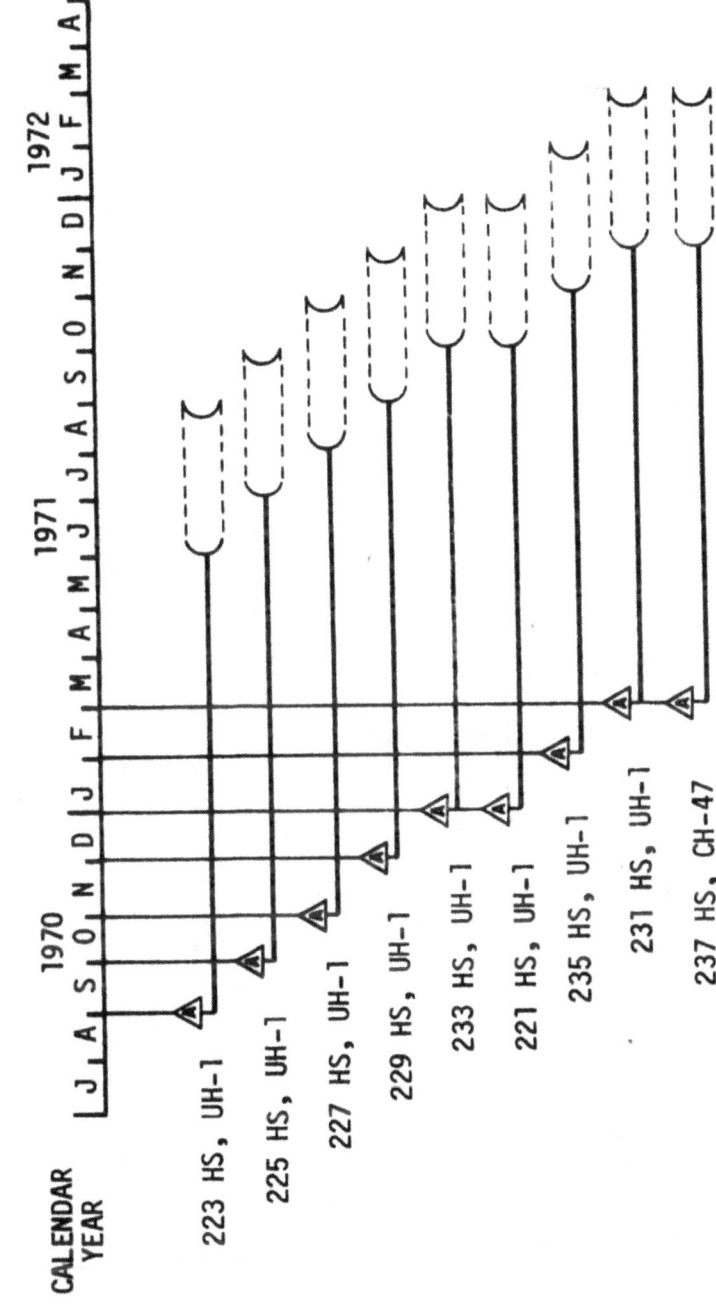

APPENDIX XI

PROGRAMMED AIRCRAFT BUILDUP
ALL TYPES OF AIRCRAFT

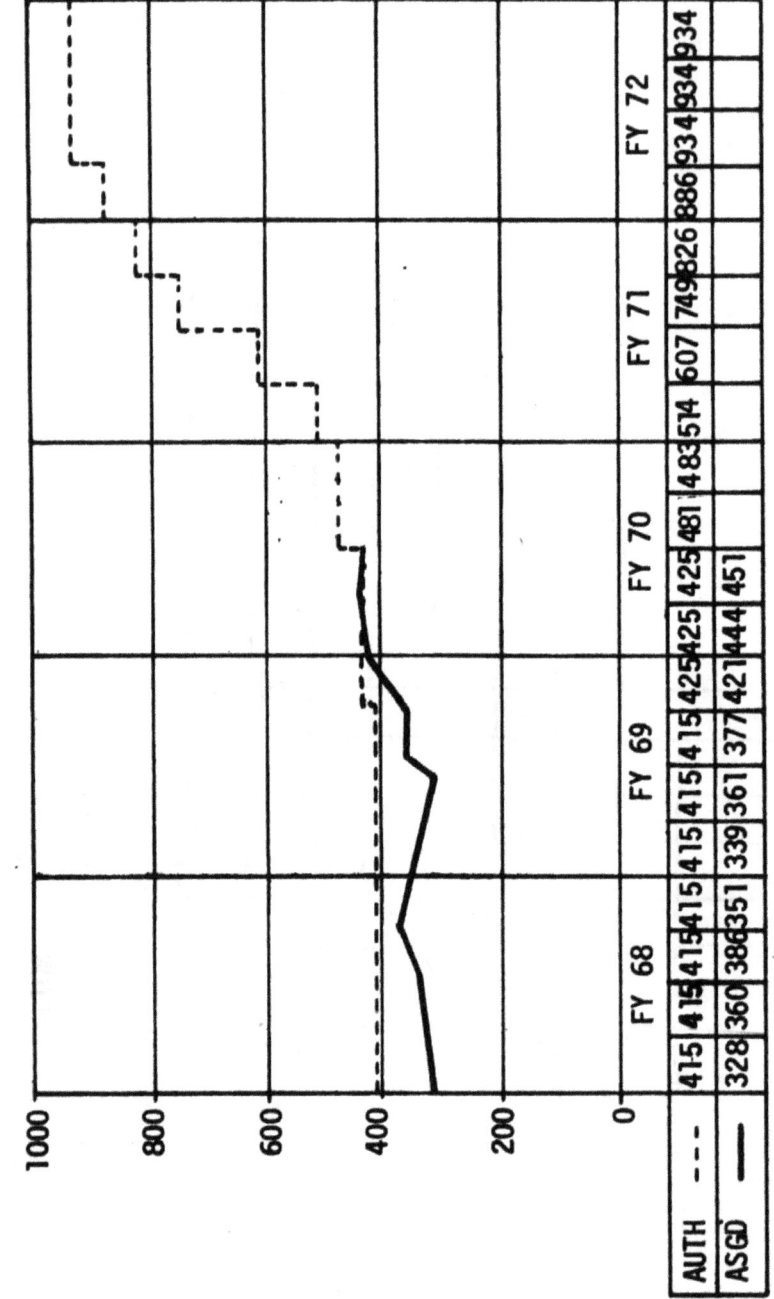

		FY 68				FY 69				FY 70				FY 71				FY 72		
AUTH - - -	415	415	415	415	415	415	415	425	425	425	481	483	514	607	749	826	886	934	934	934
ASGD ———	328	360	386	351	339	361	377	421	444	451										

SOURCE: VNAF Status Review, Jan 70

APPENDIX XII

SUMMARY OF PRESENT VNAF FORCES

TYPE AIRCRAFT	AUTHORIZED	ASSIGNED	POSSESSED	READY	FORMED	READY
		AIRCRAFT			AIRCREWS	
A-1	42	49	39	37	58	58
A-37	54	62	61	51	100	90
F-5	18	20	17	15	26	26
O-1/U-17 (Liaison)	90/40	90/32	81/31	68/27	138	136
U-17 (314th)	2	2	2	2	-	-
U-17 (12th)	-	17	17	17	19	19
T-41	18	10	10	9	-	-
H-34	25	25	24	17	26	26
UH-1	124	131	127	76	97	96
UH-1 (314th)	4	7	7	7	-	-
C-119	16	18	18	12	10	10
C47	16	21	18	16	12	12
AC-47	16	18	18	17	21	21
VC-47	4	6	6	6	-	-
EC-47	1	1	1	1	1	1
RC-47	3	3	3	3	4	4
U-6	8	9	9	9	9	9
TOTAL	481	521	489	390	521	508

SQUADRONS	TYPE OF AIRCRAFT	UE	AIRCRAFT POSSESSED	AIRCRAFT READY	CREWS FORMED	CREWS READY
2	A-1G/H	42	39	37	58	58
3	A-37	54	61	51	100	90
1	F-5	18	17	15	26	26
6	FIGHTERS	114	117	103	184	174
5	O-1	90	81	68	138	136
-	U-17	40	31	27	-	-
5	LIAISON	130	112	95	138	136
1	H-34	25	24	17	26	26
4	UH-1H	124	127	76	97	96
5	HELICOPTERS	149	151	93	123	122

APPENDIX XII (Cont'd.)

SQUADRONS	TYPE OF AIRCRAFT	UE	AIRCRAFT POSSESSED	AIRCRAFT READY	CREWS FORMED	CREWS READY
1	C-119	16	18	12	10	10
1	C-47	16	18	16	12	12
1	AC-47	16	18	17	21	21
	UH-1	4	7	7	-	-
1	VC-47	4	6	6	-	-
	U-17	2	2	2	-	-
4	TRANSPORT	58	69	60	43	43
1	U-6A	8	9	9	9	9
-	EC-47	1	1	1	1	1
-	RC-47	3	3	3	4	4
1	RECONNAISSANCE	12	13	13	14	14
1	U-17	-	17	17	19	19
-	T-41	18	10	9	-	-
1	SCHOOL SQUADRON	18	27	26	19	19

SOURCE: Aircraft & Crew Information FORSTAT, 30 Apr 70.

APPENDIX XIII

9 Jan 70

UE AIRCRAFT DELIVERIES TO VNAF
IMPROVEMENT AND MODERNIZATION PLAN

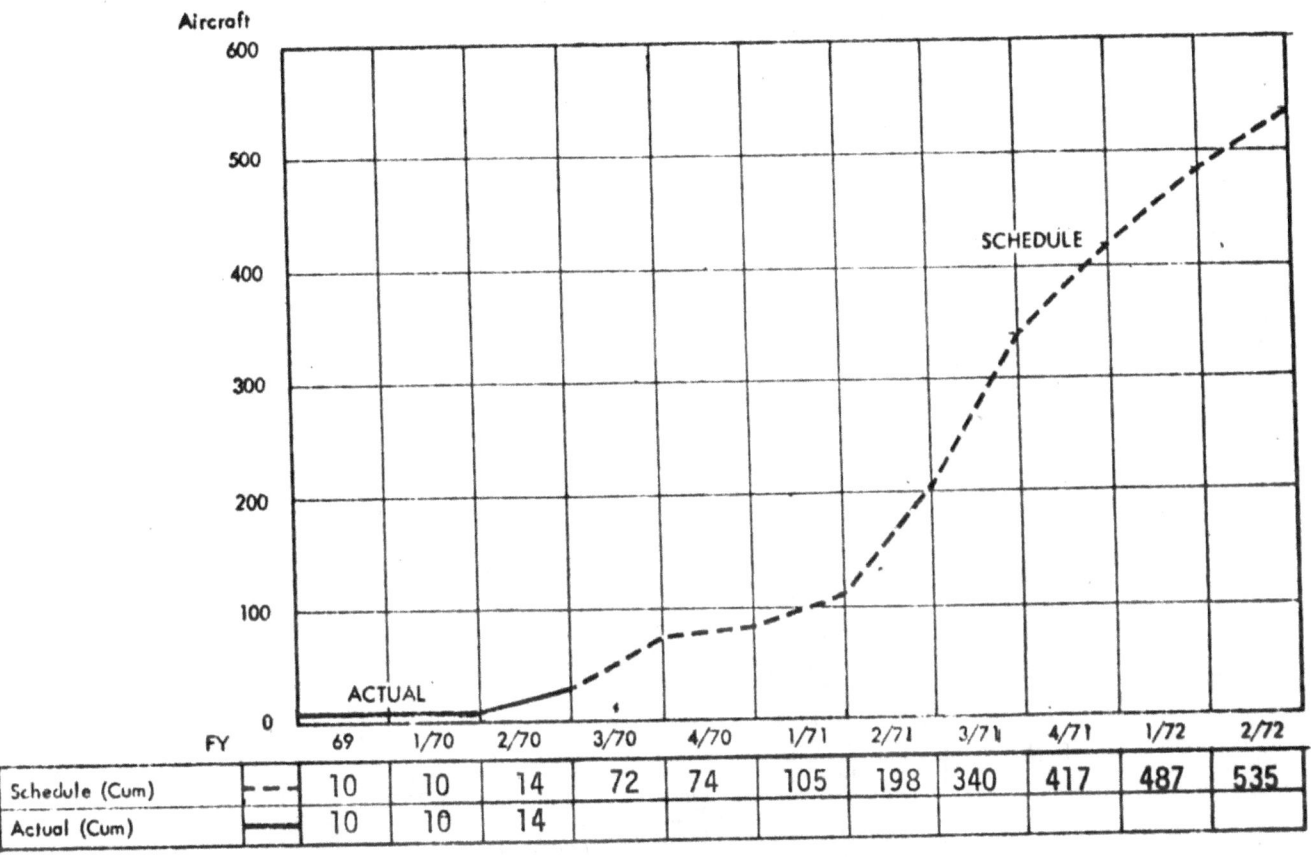

FY	69	1/70	2/70	3/70	4/70	1/71	2/71	3/71	4/71	1/72	2/72
Schedule (Cum)	10	10	14	72	74	105	198	340	417	487	535
Actual (Cum)	10	10	14								

COMMENTS:

8 T-41 A/C production schedule slipped one month.
122nd Liaison Sq being activated in FY 3/70 - Auth: COMUSMACV
2 RF-5A A/C: production schedule slipped one month.

DELIVERY SCHEDULE:

FY 69	FY 70	FY 71	FY 72
4 VC-47 A/C	4 T-41 A/C 2/70	31 UH-1H Helo 1/71	16 AC-119G A/C 1/72
4 UH-1H Helo	6 T-41 A/C 3/70	93 UH-1H Helo 2/71	18 A-37 A/C 1/72
2 U-17 A/C	10 O-1 A/C 3/70	124 UH-1H Helo 3/71	36 A-1 A/C 1/72
	44 UH-1H Helo 3/70	16 CH 47 Helo 3/71	48 C-123 A/C 2/72
	2 RF-5A A/C 4/70	4 RF-5A A/C 4/71	
	8 T-41 A/C 4/70	65 O-1 A/C 4/71	

APPENDIX XIV

UNDERGRADUATE PILOT TRAINING

TYPE OF AIRCRAFT	FY 70 [2]	FY 71 [2]	FY 72 [2]
UH-1	1,486	269	280
T-41/T-37/T-38	16	15	12
T-28	199 [3]	233	128
TOTAL UPT	1,701	517	420

TRANSITION PILOT TRAINING (CCTS)

TYPE OF AIRCRAFT	FY 70	FY 71	FY 72
F-5	10	13	10
A-37	29	64	11
C-47	35	97	113
T-28 (Instructor)	0	4	4
C-123	0	141	0
A-1	0	64	18
T-28 (Transition)	0	0	0
Other	6	6	6
TOTAL	80	389	162

OTHER TRAINING

TYPE TRAINING	FY 70	FY 71	FY 72
MAINTENANCE	1,625	2,199	82
OTHER SUPPORT	910	826	277
FY TRAINING PROGRAM COSTS ($ MILLIONS)	$38.6	$22.3	$17.9

[1] Programmed figures shown under CCTS/Transition are not necessarily additive to figures shown for Undergraduate Pilot Training.
[2] Programmed student inputs - FY 70-72.
[3] Does not include 54 carryover from FY 69.

NOTE: UH-1 helicopter training is provided by the U.S. Army. All other flying training is provided by the USAF.

APPENDIX XV

DEFENSE LANGUAGE INSTITUTE
ENGLISH LANGUAGE SCHOOL
(UH-1 PILOT TRAINING)

9 Jan 70

FY 1970

	20 Aug	3 Sep	17 Sep	1 Oct	15 Oct	29 Oct	12 Nov	26 Nov	10 Dec	24 Dec	7 Jun
ENTRIES	Class 1	Class 2	Class 3	Class 4	Class 5		Class 6	Class 7	Class 8	Class 9	Class 10
Scheduled	63	63	68	68	68		68	68	68	68	68
Cumulative	63	126	194	262	330		398	466	534	602	670
Actual	62	63	67	68	67		66	71	81	74	67
Cumulative	62	125	192	260	327		393	464	545	619	686
Number Sent to Remedial Tng	25	1	1	40	47		47	48	63	58	2

GRADUATES			Class 1	Class 2	Class 3	Class 4	Class 5		Class 6
Scheduled			63	63	68	68	68		68
▬ ▬ Cumulative			63	126	194	262	330		398
Actual			39	22	28	61	69		46
▬ ▬ Cumulative			39	61	89	150	219		265

[1] Data not available.
[2] Number in remedial training as a result of Class 10 actions not available.

APPENDIX XVI

PILOT TRAINING - VNAF
STUDENTS ENROLLED
VNAF I AND M PLAN

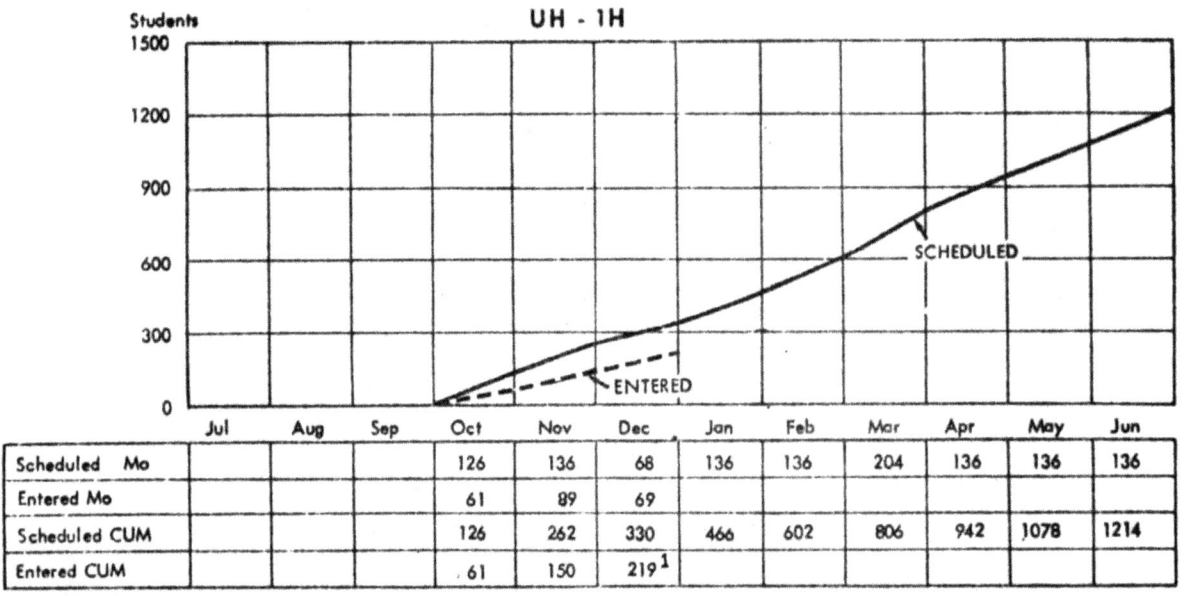

UH - 1H

	Jul	Aug	Sep	Oct	Nov	Dec	Jan	Feb	Mar	Apr	May	Jun
Scheduled Mo				126	136	68	136	136	204	136	136	136
Entered Mo				61	89	69						
Scheduled CUM				126	262	330	466	602	806	942	1078	1214
Entered CUM				61	150	219[1]						

COMMENTS: Classes enter at approximately two week intervals. Students have successfully completed the English Language School at Lackland AFB before reporting for this training.

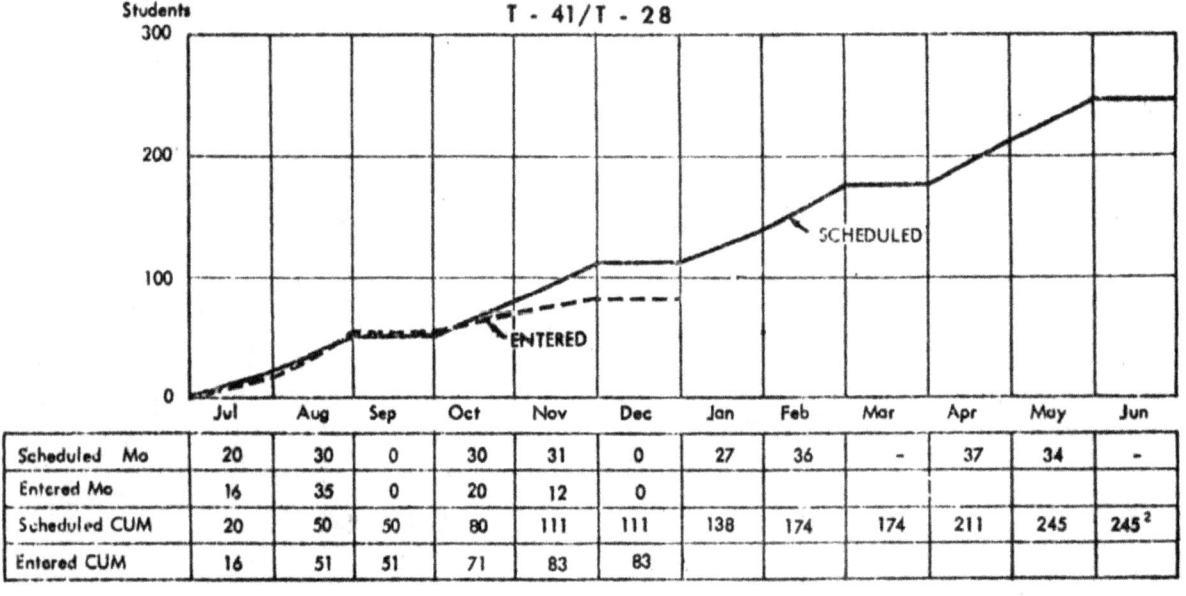

T - 41 / T - 28

	Jul	Aug	Sep	Oct	Nov	Dec	Jan	Feb	Mar	Apr	May	Jun
Scheduled Mo	20	30	0	30	31	0	27	36	-	37	34	-
Entered Mo	16	35	0	20	12	0						
Scheduled CUM	20	50	50	80	111	111	138	174	174	211	245	245[2]
Entered CUM	16	51	51	71	83	83						

SOURCE: USAF Management Summary, Jan 70
1 As of 31 Dec 69.
2 190 Total Input Requirement plus 55 from FY 69.

APPENDIX XVII

SVN ATTACK SORTIES
(VNAF, USAF, USMC, USN)

9 Jan 70

VNAF

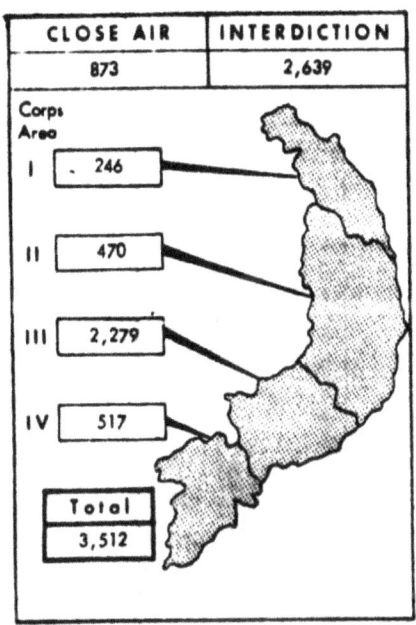

CLOSE AIR	INTERDICTION
873	2,639

Corps Area
- I: 246
- II: 470
- III: 2,279
- IV: 517

Total: 3,512

PERCENTAGE COMPARISIONS

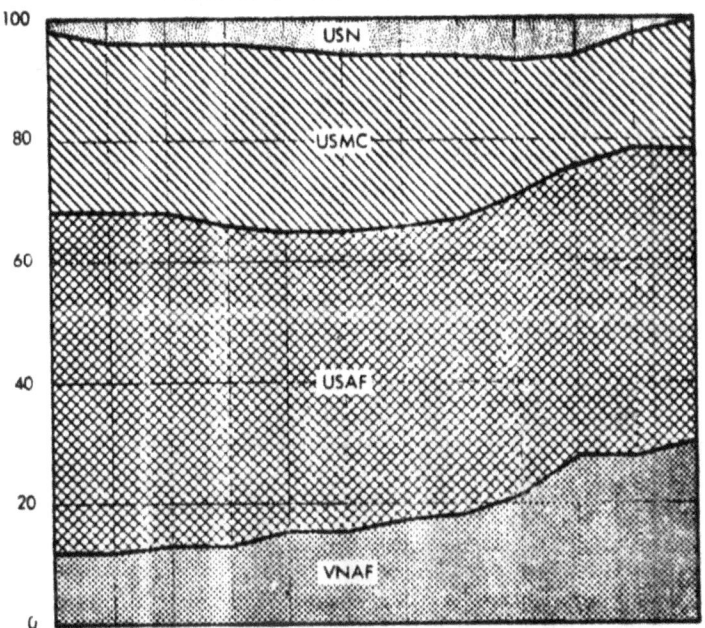

COMMENTS:

VNAF attack sorties continue to increase in RVN while US attack sorties have generally declined, the decrease in the number of SVN attack sorties flown by the USMC being the most significant. As recently as May 69, the USMC flew 30% of the total RVN attack sorties. During Nov 69, the USMC flew only 19% of the total or a reduction of 11% of the total comparing the two months.

SVN ATTACK SORTIES BY SERVICE

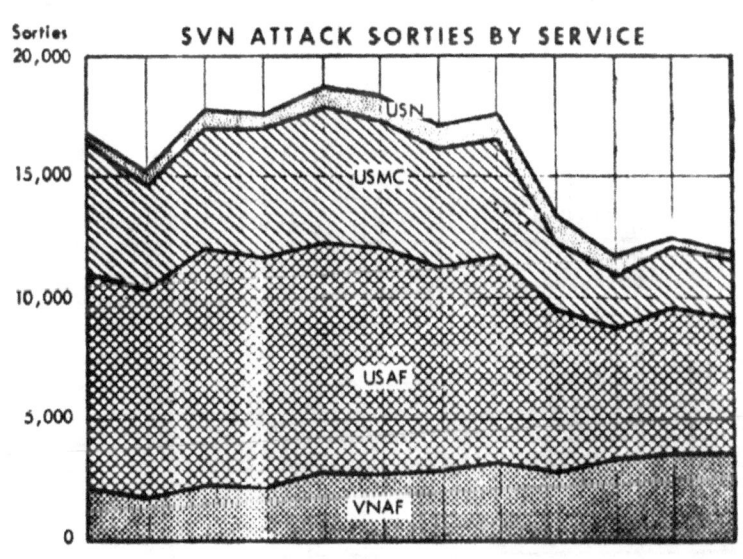

[1] Excludes B-52 Sorties

SORTIES FLOWN
APPENDIX XVIII

YEAR	TOTAL	FIGHTER	HELICOPTER	LIAISON	RECON	TRANSPORT	GUNSHIP	SCHOOL SQ
1968	164,775	31,477	101,734	12,047	5,077	6,941	-	7,499
1969	261,042	43,270	130,935	48,853	6,177	21,251	2,328	8,228
*1970	123,525	15,876	74,244	19,745	1,896	5,893	1,899	3,972

*JAN - APR 70

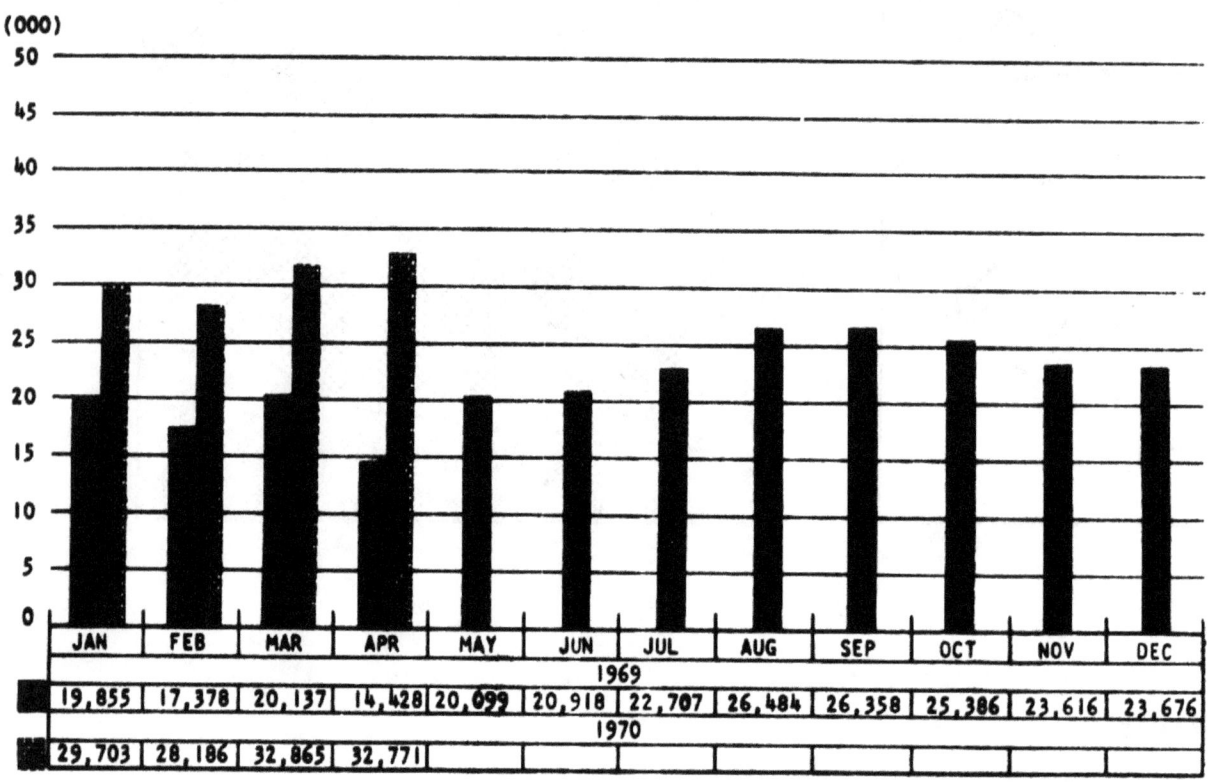

	MONTH	TOTAL	FIGHTER	HELICOPTER	LIAISON	RECON	TRANSPORT	GUNSHIP	SCHOOL SQ
1969	JAN	19,855	2,707	9,755	3,890	510	1,957	64	972
	FEB	17,378	2,723	8,752	3,184	474	1,606	58	581
	MAR	20,137	3,313	9,531	3,800	554	2,000	70	869
	APR	14,428	3,139	4,808	3,332	504	1,913	71	661
	MAY	20,099	3,718	9,141	3,851	547	1,897	64	881
	JUN	20,918	3,777	10,441	3,552	514	1,862	62	710
	JUL	22,707	3,663	11,859	3,996	575	1,820	234	560
	AUG	26,484	4,343	14,071	4,707	540	1,855	316	652
	SEP	26,358	3,751	14,153	5,161	506	1,727	279	781
	OCT	25,386	4,208	13,262	4,628	520	1,595	335	838
	NOV	23,616	3,909	12,640	4,276	470	1,470	368	483
	DEC	23,676	4,019	12,522	4,476	463	1,549	407	240
1970	JAN	29,703	4,008	17,668	4,753	479	1,534	511	750
	FEB	28,186	3,496	17,280	4,372	439	1,365	481	753
	MAR	32,865	3,986	19,666	5,340	500	1,446	429	1,498
	APR	32,771	4,386	19,630	5,280	478	1,548	478	971

SOURCE: VNAF STATUS REVIEW, 30 APRIL 1970

APPENDIX XIX

VNAF PERSONNEL STATUS-BY GRADE

GRADE	1969-72 UMD AUTHORIZED	CHANGE SINCE 31 JAN 70	28 FEBRUARY 70 ASGD	% ASGD	PROJECTED 30 DECEMBER 70 ASGD	% ASGD
GENERAL	2		-	-	-	-
LT GENERAL	1		-	-	-	-
MAJ GENERAL	15		2	13.3	2	13.3
BRIG GENERAL	40		-	-	5	12.5
COLONEL	210		23	11.0	24	11.4
LT COLONEL	649	+ 5	109	16.8	120	18.5
MAJOR	1,503	+ 50	307	20.4	316	21.0
CAPTAIN	1,889	+ 44	805	42.6	810	42.9
1ST LIEUTENANT } 2D LIEUTENANT } ASPIRANT	1,245	- 97	3,463	278.2	3,733	299.8
SUB-TOTAL	5,554	+ 2	4,709	84.8	5,010	90.2
CMSGT	1,240	+ 46	557	44.9	510	41.1
MSGT	4,390	+ 31	1,207	27.5	1,190	27.1
TSGT	2,639	+ 422	2,065	78.2	2,290	86.8
SSGT	7,459	- 66	5,768	77.3	7,620	102.2
SUB-TOTAL	15,728	433	9,597	61.0	11,610	73.8
A1C	6,856	- 44	876	12.8	3,125	45.6
A2C	3,191	- 55	2,952	92.5	3,350	105.0
A3C	3,484	- 302	2,516	72.2	10,470	300.5
AB	802	- 120	14,699	1,833.0	2,416	301.2
SUB-TOTAL	14,333	- 521	21,043	146.8	19,361	135.1
UNALLOCATED SPACES	171					
GRAND TOTAL	35,786	- 86	35,349	98.8	35,981	100.5

NOTE: THERE IS NO CORRELATION BETWEEN GRADE AND SKILL LEVEL.

SOURCE: VNAF Status Review, Feb 1970

GLOSSARY

ACW	Aircraft Control and Warning
AFAT	Air Force Advisory Team
AFGP	Air Force Advisory Group
AFLC	Air Force Logistics Command
AFSC	Air Force Systems Command; Air Force Specialty Code
ALCC	Airlift Control Center
ALO	Air Liaison Officer
ALW	Air Logistics Wing
ARDF	Airborne Radio Direction Finding
ARVN	Army of Republic of Vietnam
BDA	Bomb Damage Assessment
CINCPAC	Commander-in-Chief, Pacific Command
CJCS	The Chairman, Joint Chiefs of Staff
COMUSMACV	Commander, U.S. Military Assistance Command, Vietnam
CONUS	Continental United States
CORDS	Civil Operations and Revolutionary Development Support
CSAF	Chief of Staff, United States Air Force
CTZ	Corps Tactical Zone
CY	Calendar Year
DARN	Direct Air Request Net
DASC	Direct Air Support Center
DMZ	Demilitarized Zone
FAC	Forward Air Controller
FM	Frequency Modulation
FY	Fiscal Year
GVN	Government of Vietnam
IFF	Identification, Friend or Foe
I&M	Improvement and Modernization
IRAN	Inspection and Repair as Necessary
JCS	Joint Chiefs of Staff
JGS	Joint General Staff
KBA	Killed by Air

MAAG	Military Assistance Advisory Group
MACV	Military Assistance Command, Vietnam
MAP	Military Assistance Program
MASF	Military Assistance Service Funding
MJGS	Military Joint General Staff
NCO	Noncommissioned Officer
NORM	Not Operationally Ready-Maintenance
NORS	Not Operationally Ready-Supply
NVA	North Vietnamese Army
NVN	North Vietnam; North Vietnamese
OJT	On-the-Job Training
OR	Operationally Ready
PEC	Photo Exploitation Center
PIMO	Presentation of Information for Maintenance
PMS	Program Management System
PsyOps	Psychological Operations
Psywar	Psychological Warfare
Recon	Reconnaissance
RITS	Reconnaissance Intelligence Technical Squadron
RVN	Republic of Vietnam
RVNAF	Republic of Vietnam Armed Forces
SAMS	Special Air Mission Squadron
SEA	Southeast Asia
SEAOR	Southeast Asia Operational Requirement
TACAN	Tactical Air Navigation
TACC	Tactical Air Control Center
TACP	Tactical Air Control Party
TACS	Tactical Air Control System
TASS	Tactical Air Support Squadron
TDY	Temporary Duty
TEWS	Tactical Electronics Warfare Squadron
TOC	Tactical Operations Center
TSN	Tan Son Nhut
UE	Unit Equipment
UHF	Ultra High Frequency
UMD	Unit Manning Document
USARV	United States Army, Vietnam

VC	Viet Cong
VHF	Very High Frequency
VNAF	Vietnam Air Force
VNMC	Vietnam Marine Corps
VNN	Vietnam Navy
VR	Visual Reconnaissance